SO-EIK-653

A Generation Under Siege

Brian Stiller

VICTOR

BOOKS a division of SP Publications, Inc.

WHEATON. ILLINOIS 60187

Offices also in
Whitby, Ontario, Canada
Amersham-on-the-Hill, Bucks, England

Unless otherwise noted, Scripture quotations are from the *New American Standard Bible* (NASB), © 1960, 1962, 1968, 1971, 1972, 1973 by The Lockman Foundation, La Habra, California. Other quotations are from the *New International Version* © 1978 by the New York International Bible Society. Used by permission.

Recommended Dewey Decimal Classification: 301.431 5
   Suggested Subject Heading: ADOLESCENCE

Library of Congress Catalog Card Number: 82-062436
ISBN: 0-88207-100-9

© 1983 by SP Publications, Inc. All rights reserved
Printed in the United States of America

VICTOR BOOKS
A division of SP Publications, Inc.
P.O. Box 1825 ● Wheaton, Illinois 60187

CONTENTS

Dedicated
to my parents
Carl Hilmer and Mildred Stiller.

Within their love,
I learned to love God
and experience His world.

INTRODUCTION

I see our youth world as a city, once so prosperous, but now shut off from life. An army has surrounded it, putting it under siege.

Any attempt to document that siege is loaded with dangers. One is to overstate. Another is to generalize.

I believe there is a way out of the besieged city. In defining the problem, I also want to offer hope and suggest action to mobilize that hope into reality.

Some words of thanks are in order—to Lorna Cheetham who typed the manuscript; to Chuck Herne who helped me with the research; to my wife, Lily, who encouraged me and assisted in refining the manuscript; to our children, Murray and Muriel, who gave Dad time to "work on his book."

Thanks also to George Spaetzel for letting me use his retreat home in the Blue Mountains of Ontario. The encouragement of Tony Campolo, John Kerr, Marlene Lefever and the insights of my friend Jay Kesler have been of immeasureable help. The sharp pencil of Carole Streeter, my editor, and her belief that this book was worth the effort not only encouraged me but was a course in writing. However, I accept sole responsibility for the ideas.

I hope that this book will help you to better understand our times and our children, and then be able to do what you know you should do.

Brian Stiller
Rexdale, Ontario
1983

FOREWORD

These are tough times that require tough thinking.

We have all watched the rapid changes of our world
affect our children. But too often we fail to
understand why the changes happen.

Brian Stiller knows young people. For 20 years
he has walked and laughed and cried with them.
He has counseled them in happy times and sad.
He'd be the first to tell you he doesn't have all
the answers. But he does have some.

If you want to understand the forces shaping our kids—
If you want insight into the world of adolescence—
If you want to be part of the solution—
A Generation Under Siege is must reading!

Luis Palau
1983

1
Siege
of the Powerless

The voice on the phone signaled danger. She was almost hysterical. I talked in a gentle tone, attempting to calm her. Through the sobs and broken phrases, she told me her story....

"Brian, can you help me?

"It's too awful to even say . . . I mean . . . O God, help me!"

"Are you at home?"

"Yes, but it happened last night. . . . I can't even say the word. It's all too awful."

"Were you alone?"

"No, my dad was here. And, Brian, he's never done it before. Like he would beat me when he was drunk. I kinda got used to that. . . . But last night was so ugly. Oh, no one will ever understand!"

"I'll try . . . just tell me."

A deep sob racking her body rushed like a storm over the phone.

"Brian . . . O God, how can I ever say it?"

"Just tell me, you can trust me."

"My dad raped me. I feel so dirty . . . how can I ever look at myself in the mirror again?"

"Where was your mother?"

"She was out . . . drunk."

I heard a loud male voice in the background.

She screamed, "He's coming again! Brian, can you help me?"

A sharp crack rang out as his hand slapped against her face. The phone fell to the floor. He picked it up and slammed it back on the receiver.

I sat helpless, sick, crying out for justice. I had no name or phone number. Somewhere a teenage girl was at the mercy of a raging parent, cringing, crying, reaching for help. Someone's daughter, forever damaged, psychologically crippled, or at least scarred for life.

We are tired of seeing dying orphans in Asia, bloody massacres in El Salvador, bombed bodies in Beirut, and emaciated children in Upper Africa. We also shield our hearts from hearing the agonizing cries of children who roam our shopping plazas, wander along the streets, and fry their minds by loneliness, drugs, and crazy behavior.

I can't forget the broken heart of a nine-year-old. His frightened sister found him hanging by his belt from the bedroom door. He was one of many precious but forgotten kids muffling their hopeless sobs in the pillows of an adult society consumed with greed and personal rights. Even with the alarming rise in teenage problems, many children are being ignored, their cries simply discounted.

Western society functions by groups pressing their point by protest, power, and confrontation. But young people are without spokesmen. Their needs get lost in the unending adult agendas of family budgets, business, gay rights, right to life, crime, and on and on. Out of sight, the children are out of mind.

The adult world, fatigued with adolescent problems, is so caught up with personal issues of identity, success, and meaning that the world between three and twenty often gets lost.

Reasons

The rebellion of the 1960s erupted as young people reacted to the value systems of their parents—the establishment, big business, and centers of power. In a dramatic attempt to change not only the world but also the inner self, the youth culture formed its own path, running against the mainstream of the adult world and exploding in a frenzy of confrontation. You could see it in their lifestyles and hear it in their music.

The war in Southeast Asia convinced many adults that the communist heresy needed stopping once and for all, but young people led the revolt. The sheer size of the youth culture altered our world. The establishment became the object of attack as kids refused to believe that the adult world offered anything of real value. With Vietnam as a cause, the movement coalesced literally millions and distinct value systems emerged.

The pressure which generated the rebellion of the 1960s and 1970s died. Rather than espousing a counterview of life, young people have now bought into the value system of adults. Protesters of 10 and 15 years ago are now paying for mortgages. Apart from the normal tension created by differences in age, the two streams flow in one direction. The riverbed is materialism. The common pursuit of the good life has generated a significant measure of harmony.

Today's young people have no real hope of changing the world. The ominous problems of the nations are so huge that young people lack interest and energy to care. The faded jean is out and the designer jean is in. Kids are extending their adolescence, living at home longer, and getting married later. After all, the greatest time of freedom is during youth.

Traditionally, adulthood was seen as the time to experience freedom, unhinged from the constraints of parents. Today the average home allows such freedom that many young people choose against the risks and pressures of adulthood in favor of living at home with its security and low expense.

At the same time, adults are attempting to hold on to youthfulness—mothers attempt to look like their daughters; fathers work at keeping up with sons.

In terms of values, both groups are materialistic. Young people extend adolescence into adulthood and adults attempt to stop the clock by keeping younger. The chasm of the generation gap has been filled in. Because of this, many adults fail to see and hear the dilemma of a younger generation lacking a sense of direction.

Selfism

If the 1960s needed loud protests to challenge the abuse of power, how much more we need thinking, active, vocal youth today! The strident powers of nationalism, an overwhelming concern for self-fulfillment, the disregard for human rights by so many nations, show us a world ruled by power, as human values are crushed.

- Who hears the cries of prisoners tortured by militarism?
- Who confronts governments to rethink their armament stockpiles?
- Who challenges mindless patriotism?
- Who calls us to account for our fixation of personal greed?
- Who utters the prophetic word to a world muddling along in a strange mixture of humanism and secularism?

It surely is not our kids, and this fact is just as tragic as the silence of adults. The idealism of youth has been tarnished. The bright belief that life is to be conquered and the world to be changed is dimmed by the hassle to survive. A teenager put it clearly: "Leave the world to its own fate. Our hands are too small, our words too garbled, and our voices too subdued to make any difference."

We have turned from outer space to inner space. Bookstore shelves are lined with manuals on self-help. Christian writers advise on how to succeed in marriage, love-making, weight reduction, dealing with stress, and development of our gifts. Television preachers tell us how we can have healing and financial prosperity if we will only follow their simple formulas.

A seemingly legitimate search for the inner life is often generated by selfism—a belief that true living means finding my greatest happiness. Not only has this search spawned various cultic movements, but it has also promoted greed and narcissism.

It has also suggested that children are an economic liability. The cost to rear a child? About $100,000. A selfish search for the good life often leaves kids out of the picture. The increase in abortion isn't because those adults want to see unborn babies killed, but because they see children as a social and economic inconvenience. Babies interfere with the professional plans of the women and create economic pressures on couples. Because children are seen to serve no good purpose, many couples have simply opted out of parenthood.

I see profound implications in this loss of will. If we neglect the consequences of this displacement of human values with greed, we may reap a whirlwind. The resulting strife of this generation could become so severe as to tear away at the very fabric of our society. We dare not turn away, pretending it is simply an illusion.

Come with me. Walk the roads of our world. Set aside your personal concerns and listen. Just for a moment. It won't take long. But don't walk away until you've given yourself a chance to see and hear.

Child Abuse

She lay in the emergency ward as her father sat stonefaced in the waiting room. The cigarette burns he had inflicted were so severe that her little mind had shifted into unconsciousness to avoid the pain.

Next time you see a group of girls playing, remember that one out of ten girls has been, or soon will be, abused by an adult male. Abuse eats away at the family. Because parents have acted irresponsibly, through rage or frustration, abused kids face a foreboding future. We can't afford to wait to see how bad the long-term results will be. We have to do something now.

Pornography

An adult mind infected with increasing needs for pleasure and erotic experience may turn to children for novelty and excitement. The result is kiddie porn. In a search for titillation, a sick person will pay 600 percent more for films of children in sexual play than for adult-porn. As an industry, pornography softens social tolerance for other forms of deviant behavior. The result is more openness in sexual exploitation.

What are the implications if this is allowed to continue? Today's generation will find itself adrift morally with no horizon in view. Thousands of children will be used to feed the mills of the pornography industry. As they grow into adulthood, their emotional and psychological wounds will continue to fester.

Suicide

Suicide among 15- to 19-year-olds has increased 400 percent over the past 15 years! The torch of the 1960s, carried high in the march of life, has simply gone out. Without commitment, life falls into disrepair. Without a cause in life, selfism takes over. But that is a road without end. For if happiness is the goal of life, when does one ever become happy?

When a pursuit of happiness is combined with a personal

sense of powerlessness, the result is deadly. It isn't just the kid who has blown his mind with drugs who ends it all. Sons and daughters from stable families stun their friends and families as they quietly exit, leaving touching notes and letters—warm expressions which only add to the sting. If adults continue to withdraw from young people, they will be too far removed to see the early warnings of suicide.

Rejection

Our chosen daughter is my best little friend. She looked up at my wife one day and asked, "Why didn't my other mommy want me?" Lily responded, "It wasn't because she didn't want you, but because she wasn't able to look after you."

Now that may be too subtle a difference for her little mind to grasp. But while her wondering mind was asking the question, I could nestle her in my arms. The sorrow of rejection was being healed with the comfort of loving acceptance.

However, this is not the case for thousands of children who are simply rejected by parents who wander off to pursue their personal goals. How is a teen expected to interpret the actions of a mother or father who walks away with another partner? Regardless of what is said or what forms of compensation are given, deep to the soul comes a message which says, "I'm not really wanted."

Apathy

What is worse than rejection? To be ignored. Parents making false assumptions about kids carelessly walk way, forgetting how fragile children are, how much they need care and guidance. Parents often say:

● "My kids look and talk like adults." Many young people do look older today. Because their bodies are growing up faster, it is easy to assume that their emotional and volitional structures are also adult.

- "They are emotionally more mature than I was at their age." But possessing more freedoms does not mean they are able to handle the corresponding responsibilities.
- "They have so many more opportunities than I had." It may seem that way. But from where the kids sit, it may look like a mass of confusion.
- "They are so sophisticated. If I crowd them, I'm afraid I'll turn them off." We all need fences. It's healthy for teenagers to live within reasonable boundaries, to learn patterns of controlled behavior. The seeming sophistication of this generation does not free them from accountability.
- "Sexually, they are so well informed." It is easy to assume that kids understand the nature of sexuality. But current tragedies of both single and married youth tell of abject ignorance, both biologically and morally.

The Challenge

Yes, our children are quiet today. There are no shrill protests, just small whimpers of acquiescence. There is no confrontation, but rather a passive acceptance of their powerlessness.

Yet it was in powerlessness that our Lord came to this world. And it is with gentle love and mercy that He draws near to hurting children and parents.

When Christ was on earth, He described His mission in the prophetic words of Isaiah:

The Spirit of the Lord is upon Me,
because He anointed Me to preach the Gospel to the poor.
He has sent Me to proclaim release to the captives,
And recovery of sight to the blind,
To set free those who are downtrodden,
To proclaim the favorable year of the Lord (Luke 4:18-19).

This book is a call to adults who are not part of the prevailing currents in our society—that together we may reach to children in despair with the care and love of Christ.

2
Children
of the Ghetto

It was late as Hank quietly slipped upstairs. Mom would be sleeping and he didn't want to disturb her. But she was awake.

"Hank, please come here for a moment," she called. He went into her bedroom and immediately sensed something was wrong.

Hank's dad had left a few years ago. Recently his mom had been dating another man.

"Hank," his mom said, "we plan to get married." Hank was pleased. This would be a good deal for Mom. But he wasn't ready for the bombshell.

"Hank, there is something else you need to know." He looked up, confused by the threat of danger.

"There is one condition. He only wants me. You see, Hank, soon you will be finishing high school and then you'll go on to college, and then what will there be for me? Oh, Hank, you do understand, don't you?"

Hank understood all right. That Christmas he walked away from the only parent he had thought loved him.

The trauma of family dislocation unnerves kids and leads

them to equate marriage with hurt, loneliness, and failure. The wounds of rejection may never heal into scars, but just continue to fester.

A small town in Ontario, with a school of 700 students, was shocked in 1981 when within a few months, five students committed suicide. Not one death was drug-related. The parents were frightened, for there seemed to be no ready explanation.

Many of our young people are under attack. Adults are sending them confusing and contradictory signals that disorient their rational powers. Instead of learning how to make clear decisions, they huddle helplessly in their silent ghettos.

A ghetto is a world closed to the outside. When it is under siege, the enemy shuts off nourishment and assistance until the people in the ghetto starve or surrender. Because they have nowhere to turn, they are intimidated by their own sense of powerlessness.

The youth in our society have gone through exhausting upheavals over the past 25 years. Because the 1960s were noisy, parents recognized something was wrong. Today an even greater upheaval is occurring. Yet it is so silently unobtrusive that parents and societal leaders are complacent. Their response, "Oh sure, our kids are having some problems, but so what? Every generation has its problems."

This indifference reinforces the aloneness in the ghetto. The very people who could halt the siege on the teenage ghetto are so caught up in their own crises that they fail to recognize the signs.

For most adolescents, this means that necessary nutrients for healthy growth of body, mind, and spirit continue to be cut off. The young are consigned to existence in their ghettos of youth culture without guidance, without meaning, without emotional nourishment.

Because families are smaller, often with both parents working, children have more money available. As if in response, the drug culture has created a growing network of suppliers and dealers. Who is the logical market? The middle-class suburban teenager who has the dollars to pay for the drugs.

Another factor affecting teenagers is the lack of religious faith and moral values among adults. As people move away from church involvement, they have nothing beyond remembered moralizing from their parents to pass on to their children. You have heard the comment, "I'll let my kids decide for themselves if they want to go to church." Do those parents let a seven-year-old decide if he should play in the street?

A prime example of the demise of our moral foundations is in the indiscriminate practice of abortion. The real purpose of abortion on demand is to alleviate the social inconvenience of bearing or providing for a child. This is part of the moral climate in which our youth are being raised!

We live in constant tension. Two major issues facing our communities in the 1980s are unemployment and hopelessness. The sense of hopelessness paralyzes and drives us into personal indulgence or cynicism.

Too many people today believe they are simply the result of their past. Yet to conclude this as the end of the matter is to deny reality. For we are, in fact, the products of our future. We can become what we see ourselves to be. We are formed, as of yesterday, by our past. But today we are being changed by hope of who we see ourselves to be tomorrow. A new day will dawn. A new birth is due soon. We are "between a death and a difficult birth" (Samuel Beckett).

Change

I was raised in a prairie parsonage, the second youngest of five children. Life was very uncomplicated, lines clearly drawn. We lived in the same area for a number of years. My brothers and sisters and I all went to the same schools. The roles of Mom and

Dad were clear. There was sufficient control so that dating a girl meant my dad would know her dad. Because my father was a minister, the girl's father would think I was a good risk. What a camouflage!

But the world as I knew it changed in the 1960s as people believed that two saviors, science and education, would solve individual and national problems. This optimism stimulated corporate, educational, and governmental growth.

Many parents, clergymen, politicians, and teachers were absolutely mystified as a growing discontent erupted in the Free Speech movement. They did not recognize that abundance and sophistication cannot satisfy the deeper needs of students. Nor that they could not control the actions of young people determined to challenge and change the basis on which society was constructed.

The 1960s were characterized by searching. Highways were lined with young people who had "hit the road." A Harvard credentialed high priest of drug culture led countless thousands into mind trips.

What baffled sociologists was that many of these young people were from "good" homes. And yet that was the point. Parents were so consumed with providing "good" education and "good" material advantages that they misunderstood the gut issues. Prosperity does not answer the age-old questions: "Who am I? What am I worth? Where am I going?"

In reaction to adult materialism, young people developed a counterculture with its own set of values and symbols. We saw these in their music, hair, clothing, recreation, entertainment, songs and heroes. The rhetoric of songs and speeches was clearly antiestablishment.

In the 1970s, the protestors married and began to pay mortgages. The powerful songs of searching degenerated into noisy, acid rock that expressed confusion and disintegration. The search was over. Mistrust was in. Watergate became the symbol of hypocrisy in high places. "If you can't trust your leader, whom can you trust?"

The search for truth was diminished by the pressure of finding a secure job. World issues were understood, but they had become so gigantic that attempts to deal with them seemed irrelevant, and so the youth society turned its attention inward. Apart from a mild interest in human rights and nuclear power, their outward concern was dramatically transferred into finding personal peace and prosperity.

Charles A. Reich, in his prophetic *The Greening of America,* asked why the system went wrong. "The first crucial fact is the existence of a universal sense of powerlessness. We seem to be living in a society that no one created and no one wants" (Random House, p. 8).

The switch of concern from the world to self generated a surprising movement, as adults pressed for an egalitarian society. It began with the women's rights movement and spread to rights for children and workers; then to freedom of information, guaranteed minimum wage; to civil rights, and then rights for gays. This switch from outer space to inner space produced what the sociologists called the Me Generation.

Five Characteristics

None of us lives in a bell jar. Society inevitably affects our children. The issues of this age influence the way young people form values, make choices, and establish patterns for life.

By the time a person is 16 or 17, the influence of parents is lessened as the peer group, with its subtle forms of persuasion, takes over. Few young people want to be thought of as odd, and so to measure up to the expectations of their group, they conform. A fad begins in a small group and then expands. If it fits with broader cultural values, it may become a trend that changes the fabric of society.

Every age expresses its deep feelings and expectations

through ideas and movements. The following characteristics may help you better understand the conflicting influences that isolate so many young people in emotional, intellectual, and spiritual ghettos.

• Supernaturalism. Naturalism was the predominant philosophical view in universities well into the 1960s. The scientific method ruled supreme. Arguments to convince students of the validity of Christian faith were based on the rational structure of Christianity and the proven accuracy of the Bible. Cynicism prevailed and unbelief was the norm. Religion lacked credibility. Asking students to attend a religious event was like asking them to commit intellectual or social suicide.

Today, in contrast, we see religious gullibility. The switch is from refusal to believe to willingness to believe—in almost anything. This leaves many young people vulnerable to non-Christian religions and cults. Experience has become the acid test for truth. If it feels good, how can it be wrong? In their personal search for identity and meaning, these students screen the various forms of religious experience only by the satisfaction they give.

Cult leaders recognize this unguarded tendency, and recruit people who are lonely, disoriented, without purpose, highly idealistic, and looking for some form of spiritual meaning.

This move toward supernaturalism comes from:

—A need for religious experience, the roots of which are deeper than mysticism, liturgy, or rational and logical statements about God.

—A felt need for group identity and security. Religious group experience provides not only a place to discover truth but a secure setting in which to find inner stability. This intense, inner longing for personal significance is validated and then expressed in the religious group.

• Passivism. During the 1950s young people were passive because they simply were not aware of the issues. Today they have every opportunity to be up-to-date with national and international affairs but instead have withdrawn. The problems are so large that any effort they could make seems irrelevant. "What can anyone do?" becomes the hackneyed question.

This mood was dramatically confronted by Terry Fox, a 21-year-old, who had lost a leg to cancer. He resolved to run across Canada on one good leg and one artificial leg and raise money for cancer research. His step-by-step courage and determination as he crossed the continent made him front-page news. After running to Thunder Bay, almost halfway across Canada, he had to return to his home in Vancouver, because there were further signs of cancer.

Canada responded with over 23 million dollars in contributions to the Terry Fox Fund. After his death, an annual Terry Fox Day was established. One young man with a vision and physical determination broke through the passivity of youth. He had dared to confront cancer, bringing it to public attention.

Our society is in need of heroes. Egalitarianism has set in. But this mood of equal rights for all leads not to equality but to sameness. A push toward equal rights leaves able people reluctant to excel or to rise to leadership. The message is, "Survive and care about yourself." However, achieving this personal security creates a deadening conformity.

● Narcissism. Narcissus, a statuesque god in Greek mythology, was so utterly taken with himself that he spent his life in self-idolization. One day while adoring his reflection in a pool, he fell in and drowned.

Young people today tend toward privatism, retreating from the vulnerabilities of "out there" and embarking on a journey inward. Self-fulfillment has taken over as they work to buy stereos, exotic trips, expensive clothes and fun. A sense of their inability to make any impact on the larger problems of life, combined with an insecurity about the future, has created the advertising line, "Get all the gusto you can get."

A life caught up in self-fulfillment, pleasure, and inner peace eclipses the outside world with its needs. Energy needed for healthy personal growth is snuffed out in the drive for hedonistic self-preservation. In a world of both starvation and obesity, our children learn a worldview of getting the best for themselves.

• Authoritarianism. As life becomes more complex, as fragile international relations move from crisis to crisis, as the infrastructures of our own society shake loose, and as leaders are unable to offer substantial solutions, young people increasingly look for a convincing authority figure.

Dr. Jay Kesler, President of Youth for Christ/U.S., believes teenagers have a growing interest in hearing the stories of older people. In their fear of making personal mistakes, they back away from personal risk and want to listen to what others have done. This way they are able to vicariously live through the experience of others without the vulnerability of risk.

An outgrowth of the need for authority is a new form of legalism. As a person subjects himself to a leader with answers, he is given a formal or legal code which all group members are called on to follow. This provides the leader with continuing control. The follower tends to feel secure, not realizing that "Trust me and I'll answer your questions" is often followed by "Obey me."

This legalism is found in cults; the leader is the final arbiter and court of law, and members must fall into line with his reasoning and commands.

• Romanticism. A young person's need for satisfying emotional experiences can dominate all dimensions of living. The ideal of love as a warm feeling has been legitimized by leading members of society, as musicians, writers, movie stars and other celebrities have redefined the term. . . . Self-interest, personal fulfillment, and pleasure form the basis for a love relationship. . . . Life is best lived when *I* get what *my* desires demand. . . . The urge for sexual gratification is stepped up.

The genuine romance in finding a life partner and building a stable future together can be pushed aside in the search for a relationship that will make *me* feel good.

Although the word *love* is still used, the meaning is different. Love as an expression of the will to act responsibly toward and for the loved one has been changed to mean a feeling of self-gratification. When *she* is beautiful and makes *me* feel as *I* want to feel, it must be love.

Conclusions

These characteristics form the basis of the adolescent culture today. Supernaturalism discourages the young person from being selective in religious experience. Thus the desperate search for inner meaning can be easily manipulated by self-serving cultists and leaders. The tendency to move away from societal problems leaves our youth easily persuaded by anyone who can demonstrate he has the answers. This passive rather than active response doesn't indicate a lack of awareness, but rather a conviction that nothing can be done.

This passive response to our present world order leads them to focus on their needs. If they can't do anything about the problems that surround them, they tend to shut off the needs of others and be concerned with themselves.

Narcissism probably characterizes this generation more than any other word. The search for religious experience combined with a passive response leaves them vulnerable to authority figures. They open their arms to charismatic leaders who appear to have all the answers.

Alvin Toffler, author of *Future Shock* and *The Third Wave,* comments, "We've hit a dangerous level of pessimism just now. When we start to believe that there is no way out . . ., we fall into inertia. And that opens the way to totalitarianism."

A city under siege is faced with four options: give in to the enemy, starve, find a way out, or wait for help from outside.

Those under siege usually think in terms of the first three options. Outside help is hardly considered. Our culture has turned away from Christian thinking. We have so long been nourished by secular thought that many of us think only within the confines of human adequacy.

The adults of the 1980s have unwittingly aided the siege against their own children.

3
Dying Families

The idea of Christmas seemed so wonderful. The shopping center was ablaze with lights. Shoppers were tired, but the excitement was there. Suzie's job was to close up the candy kiosk, count the money, and make the deposit. She really didn't want to go home. Last Christmas was so different. . . . What was there to go home to tonight? A year can change everything!

When she finished work, she waited in the swirling snow for the bus. It finally arrived and took her to a block from the apartment she shared with her mother. Last Christmas she lived in a house with her mom and dad and two brothers.

When she got to the building, she waited for an elevator. At last the door opened and two screaming kids pushed their way past her. Lurching and groaning, the elevator made its way up to the seventh floor. Picking up her bags, Susie walked slowly down the hall.

The lump in her throat got bigger. The few dollars she earned were hardly enough to buy her clothes, let alone a Christmas present for Mom. She wondered how her brothers were doing— they lived with her father across town. A tear rolled down her face as she fumbled with the lock. Suzie flicked on the light, dropped her bags, and sat down at the kitchen table, alone. The tears ran more quickly now. The cry was there, but no one heard.

Suzie is just one of millions. Put them together in an arena, and the combined cries would rise like the noise of a rock concert. But we don't hear them that way. Their muffled cries sound alone, behind closed doors.

Changing Families

My childhood home was quite the opposite. As the fourth of five children, I grew up with a very clear understanding of what Dad did, what Mom did, and the boundaries of my freedom. I could not have imagined Dad having interest in another woman, and I concluded that Mom was fulfilled as a mother and wife. Comparing my childhood of the 1950s to being a parent in the 1980s, I ask the question, "Whatever happened to the family?"

My childhood memories are pleasant. I tested the boundaries of my freedom and quickly found the holes under the fence. Some left enough room for an easy exit. In other places the barbed wire snagged. Mom and Dad saw the tear. Sometimes they could be fooled, but not often. Today I see bewildered looks from parents and young people when I ask about their families.

For us to understand the siege that is slowly starving so many families, we must go back to the postwar period and follow the changes that have taken place.

Until the early part of this century, our communities were made up of somewhat isolated, independent, and self-sufficient families. Many worked on farms, producing enough food for themselves and generating sufficient income to purchase necessary goods and services.

Yet some found the self-sufficient lifestyle of the farm more a nightmare than a dream. So as World War I brought technological changes, many moved from farm and rural communities into cities. With jobs offering secure wages and predictable hours, it seemed more appealing to live in town.

Urbanization continued. Societal and individual life reorganized. In joining the assembly line, breadwinners exchanged managing their own enterprises with making secure wages. During World War II, women went out to work. Although they often did the same work as men, they were paid much less. The fighting spirit of women for equal rights was being lit—a flame that would be fanned during the 1960s.

Postwar urban living in the 1950s and 1960s produced an increased affluence and the growth of the middle class. It also produced overcrowding, less work for children, more opportunity for delinquent behavior, and a real loss of individual identity and purpose.

The family was being redesigned. In earlier decades, families had been economic units, working together. Children were seen as economic assets. But by 1950, Father left in the morning and returned in the evening. There was little chance for his children to understand his job, let alone his total person. When Father could no longer be observed at work, the model for working was weakened.

In addition, most parents were unable to put children to work, since they no longer had farms or family businesses. That meant they couldn't supervise the process of learning how to work. Many parents, dissatisfied with the status of their own employment, wanted their children to improve themselves by education. Better education meant better jobs.

Then the baby boom hit and children crowded our schools. Education was given more money and attention. Parents who had known the economic depression of the 1930s, and the horrors of war, were determined this new generation would get what they had missed. Nothing was spared, since it never occurred to them that their children would reject the values they had lived and fought for.

The family continued to change into the 1970s. The emerging counterculture of youth challenged the myth of success, leaving parents bewildered. Antiestablishment rallies focused the latent hostility of youth to adults, as they questioned Western domination, the value of education, corporate power, and the criteria of success. This hostility personalized as sons and daughters challenged their parents, who had believed that by hard work they were providing good things for their children.

This was a time of knowledge explosion. Scientists were beginning to play with the genetic code. Nuclear proliferation threatened the physical isolation of North America. Former allies of the Western World were vacillating.

The antimaterialism of youth was leading them to search for truth and meaning. In reaction to the values and lifestyles of their parents, many young people began tripping on a variety of drugs. This led to further alienation between parents and children. To most parents, alcohol was a much more acceptable drug because they understood it; other forms represented all that was repulsive and frightening.

One surprise was the renewal of religious interest, particularly the Jesus Movement, which brought religious events and discussions into all sectors of the community. The Jesus Movement became especially visible as actors, sports figures, singers, writers, and politicians testified to their newfound faith.

The family continued to change. The child was now even less essential. Working mothers found a new sense of independence and self-worth. Extramarital affairs were no longer an opportunity solely for the husband. Teenagers were working, allowing for less contact with the parents. Increasingly, family meals were eaten in shifts. Cars gave teenagers independence, less time with parents and more with peers.

These newfound freedoms did not bring fulfillment. Instead they encouraged divorce, suicide, incest, and alienation. The dream of many parents—two cars, fun-filled holidays, good education, and substantial retirement income—was shattered. As parents split up, single-parent families became a growing reality. Inflation ate away at savings. Homosexual advocates demanded the acceptance of gay marriages. Live-in marriage was seen as a viable alternative.

Modern Families

The traditional family is now a minority. A recent survey in Toronto found that the family of stay-at-home mother, working-outside-the-home father, and one or more children, made up only 20 percent of the 539,570 families. In 25 percent of families, with children under 18 years of age living at home, both parents were working. Forty-six percent of the families had no children under 18 living at home. It is estimated that within five years, up to 20 percent of Canadian families will choose to be childless. Eight percent of the families are now single-parent. The U.S. shows a 79 percent increase in single-parent families since 1970. (Benjamin Schlesinger, *The One Parent Family,* University of Toronto Press).

A birthrate of 2.1 children per woman is needed to maintain population. In 1959, the rate was 3.9 per woman. By 1976 it was 1.8. As the family becomes smaller, greater demand is placed on each child to succeed.

The two-income family is precipitating change. Over half of married couples are both working outside the home. In only 24 percent of families is the father the sole breadwinner. Many factors influence this rise in employed women: the growth of clerical and service sectors drawing more women into the labor market, later marriages, declining birthrates, better and varied education, a change in attitudes toward women working outside the home, and rising costs. The price of housing alone makes it almost impossible for the family to survive on one income. For some, the desire for the good life pushes both into working.

Single-parent families tend to get the short shrift. In the U.S., one-third are headed by women below the poverty line. Of these, over one-half hold paid jobs in addition to their family duties. In Canada, one in ten families is headed by a single parent. Of these, 85 percent are managed by women. One-half are below the poverty line and of these, 98 percent are on welfare. Single-parent families now constitute about 40 percent of welfare budgets in most Canadian provinces (Ann Silversides, "The Catch-22 of Single Parents on Welfare," *Macleans,* November 17, 1980).

A recent survey showed that 33 percent of women over 18 feel that their attempt to advance in the marketplace will be the major area of social conflict in the future. In the rural province of Saskatchewan, only one percent of teenage girls plan to choose homemaking as their vocation.

Some students see the traditional family as demeaning, a senseless component of society. A group of British social scientists said, "Do away with the family, because it is a primary conditioning device for a Western imperialist worldview."

Divorced Families

All of these conditions and attitudes have contributed to the breakup of the modern family. When the bands of marital commitment finally snap under the tension, the psyches of children and young people are torn apart by parents who decide they can no longer live together.

Elisa arrived home late. She had had a good time with her friends, but the nagging dilemma at home didn't go away even at the party. Her mom and dad didn't hear her enter, since they were having one of their arguments. The marriage was over— the constant hostility was more than either could bear. This dispute centered on who would get what in the settlement.

When Elisa heard her name mentioned, she listened more closely. At first it felt good to hear them arguing over who would get her. But her interest turned to horror as she realized they were debating about who would have to take her. To either parent, she would be a burden.

Elisa was crushed and she reacted. Her broken heart could stand it no longer. She ran to the basement and found her father's hunting gun. She remembered how it worked from when they went on duck hunts near the sloughs outside their prairie city. She brushed away a tear in her hurried search for shells. Finding one, she jammed it into the 12-gauge shotgun.

Her parents screamed as the shot rang out. Together they stumbled into the basement, horrified at the realization that their argument had been heard. Elisa's shattered head and the blood-spattered wall told the story.

In the U.S. there are over 11 million children under the age of 18 whose parents are divorced. In Canada, it is over one million. Fifty-four percent of children born this year will be living with just one of their parents before they reach the age of 18 (*Listening to America's Families,* White House Conference on the Family, October 1980).

Divorce produces a variety of emotional responses. After the initial shock, it is followed by "depression, denial, anger, low self-esteem and among pre-teens, the feeling that somehow they are responsible. They are old enough to realize what is going on, but don't have adequate skills to deal with it," commented Dr. J. Tedesco, chief psychologist, Child Guidance Center, Des Moines, Iowa.

As children grow older they become more sophisticated in their attempts to deal with the separation. Often one parent plays the emotions of the child off against the other parent. A study on 72 divorced, middle-class families showed that boys suffer the most, receiving less support from their mothers. Because they are male, teachers and parents expect more from them (Benjamin Schlesinger, *The One Parent Family*).

Financial burdens are heavier for the divorced, as they move from supporting one home to two. The myth, "Two can live as cheaply as one" didn't work for the couple and so the two-income family evolved. Now, separation and divorce force two homes to live off the same support. If money was a cause of frustration before, it becomes a larger source of tension and aggravation.

A divorced woman, facing the reality of insufficient income, moved across town with her three children and lived with her mother in a one-bedroom house. The financial stress multiplied the complexity. The children not only lost their father, home, and neighborhood, but also school and friends. It was a major social and psychological shock for them. The tender plants had been torn up by the roots. The transplant, lacking tender, loving care, didn't hold.

Legal battles only add to the stress of divorce. As parents negotiate for custody, the courts are caught in a no-win situation. And children hear and see the pent-up hatred of their parents—as yet another memory picture of marriage and home.

The most damaging result of marriage breakdown is the loss of personal esteem and self-worth. When the marriage breaks, regardless of the cause, a sense of failure and loss of confidence occurs. Being alone compounds with identity crisis to lead women to a variety of problems. For many, welfare is degrading. Money tensions put pressure on the kids. A simple thing like buying a gift so Susy can go to Mary's birthday party becomes a problem. If ice skating costs 50¢ and isn't in the budget, it is out.

Studies on the moral orientations of children without fathers showed:

● Father-absent boys tend to resist blame when caught doing something wrong.

● Alone, they are not able to judge or identify moral implications involving crime and trust.

● They rate "moral values" as less important than do other

children. This includes consideration for others and obedience to the rules.

• They feel less guilt in their reactions to situations where cheating in competition or death due to negligence occur.

• They engage in more aggressive behavior—threatening or actual physical attacks and verbal expressions of anger (Benjamin Schlesinger, *The One Parent Family*).

Children from broken homes cause a strikingly disproportionate share of discipline problems in school and fare worse academically than their peers from two-parent homes.

A study by the Charles Kettering Foundation examined the behavior and achievements of 18,244 children from grades 1 to 12, selected from many economic and social levels. Comparing father-absent families to two-parent families, the ratios were 9 to 5 in dropouts and 8 to 1 in expulsions from school.

The present crisis becomes even more critical when we realize that the early experiences of a child determine many of the meanings he gives to his adult life. His early years form the inner picture. His adult life is a blow-up of that picture.

A conscience is a sensitive instrument, finely tuned to respond to stimuli and then to make moral choices. During childhood, the conscience develops the capacity to select and discriminate. A child accumulates a repertoire of experience which teaches him how to work and play. So much of that repertoire comes from watching parents relate to each other, to their community, relatives, and peers. For example, our adult attitudes toward authority find their roots in our early experiences. A just father will tend to produce in his child an understanding for justice. A child who is raised under an irrational parent will develop a distorted picture of authority and justice.

Each child has a darkroom hidden in his inner self. Pictures are taken and developed and looked at to make sense out of life, to decide what is right and wrong, and to answer questions like,

"Who am I?" When fighting parents and divorce are added to this photo album, the child may picture himself as rejected.

Father usually becomes the absent parent, although there is a slight trend toward giving custody to fathers. This separation from the father often triggers a child's apathy and lack of motivation. Studies by A. M. Nicholi II of Harvard Medical School show the following responses in children without fathers in the home:

• A rageful protest over desertion

• A denial of that loss and an increased fantasy with the departed parent

• Efforts at reunion

• Irrational guilt and an expressed need for personal punishment

• Exaggerated anxieties over the separation and increased fear of being abandoned

• A decrease in ability to control impulse.

The absence of the father often leads to a drop in the child's motivation for achievement, inability to defer immediate gratification for later reward (a sign of immaturity), low self-esteem, and an increased susceptability to the growing peer influence and delinquency (Armand Nicholi II, "Absent Parents, Troubled Children," *Pastoral Renewal,* May 1980, Vol. 4, No. 11).

Causes

A number of factors have contributed to this shift in family life:

• Divorce is so easy to get. Church leaders, sports figures, and government people slip from one relationship to another. For a few, divorce is the only viable solution; those are not the ones who give me major concern. My concern is about those who for superficial reasons have chosen to break up. As these adults refuse to exercise their wills to resist the 20th-century plague of self-interest, they are sending a message to young people entering marriage—if it doesn't meet your fantasies and further your self-interest, just split.

• The family pattern is affected by more and more women working outside the home. Economic pressures in the home often require both parents to work outside the home. This puts additional demands on the mother to continue to meet the emotional needs of the children, look after the house, plus keep up with her job. Her schedule can create an emotional overload. The immediate impact may be the breakdown of her relationships with both children and husband. A child arriving home from school to an empty house may sense a lack of security. And the child may feel hostility toward the mother, because she is too fatigued to hear the cry for attention.

The search for significance has led many women to conclude that this is best found outside the home. Some social observers believe that the role of the wife and mother working at home is passé. Smaller families, more conveniences, and less physical labor have made more time available for Mother. Female students are choosing professions they are reluctant to set aside for motherhood.

• Family mobility greatly affects a child's sense of belonging. To an adolescent, friends are very important. There is a stability in family roots being put down into the soil of a community which helps to create a sense of belonging. A child knows who his friends are. He knows which neighbors will get angry if the baseball lands in their gardens.

If the child or teenager is uprooted too many times, he may experience a loss of belonging. Some children adapt, while others may actually mourn the loss of their friends. Fathers who seek moves for better employment, status, and economic advantage sometimes fail to see the impact of this on children. Rather than the job being the means of supporting the family, the job becomes number one, and the family is forced to fall into second place.

● Television's impact has not yet been fully measured. Parental preoccupation has made TV a time-filler. For the smaller child, it actually becomes the baby-sitter. As the child grows into adolescence, television significantly interferes with the child's need for learning how to relate to family and friends. Television mediates reality for the child. Rather than experiencing situations firsthand, the child deals with nature, adventure, problem-solving, and relationships via the media. Television interprets reality and then tells the child how to deal with it. It thus decreases motivation for the child to launch out into personal exploration and primary contacts.

● A common trait among adolescents is the lack of ability to control impulses. Permissive reaction to the old school of discipline was based on the belief that to restrict a child's self-expression was to repress his creative drive. In overreacting, educators and trendsetters discounted the value of controls.

Controls are not necessarily restrictive; in fact, they can be freeing. A controlled child can focus his energy rather than diffusing it on nonproductive impulses.

One reason for the educators' misjudgment was their failure to distinguish between a creative child and an undisciplined child. There is evidence that we are returning to a more disciplined approach to childrearing. But, in the meantime, we continue to live with a generation of young people, many of whom have not experienced an environment of restraint and personal control.

Up to middle adolescence, the primary model for learning is the parent. Early in life, the child will try to act like the parent, as he copies attitudes and values. If the parent is absent, he or she will be replaced by another model. It has been estimated that the average time a father spends with a child per day is 37 seconds. A child can easily interpret this as rejection, which can breed hostility or contempt for the father.

There are many positive changes in the family in recent years.

For example: The family is now smaller, allowing for more individual attention to children. Mothers are freed from stereo-typing roles, giving them opportunities they deserve.

However, both positive and negative changes have come so quickly that we seem unable to make the adjustment. Has the family become an endangered species? In what form will it survive? Old forms are dying and new designs are surfacing. We can't afford to turn back the clock to the days of ten children. Many mothers will continue to work outside the home. What matters now is the development of new structures which are founded on trust, commitment, fidelity, and love. Home should be a place where children can grow to emotional and spiritual health.

What Can a Parent Do?

There are positive initiatives parents can take in developing new patterns:

• The family is the place where children become like their parents. Within your complex agenda—financial security, job enhancement, use of personal gifts, and the unending search for fulfillment—see that your daily schedule allows you suffi-cient time to express love to your partner, to play with your children, and to work at building your home.

• In your home, make choices based on what you believe to be true. This assumes that you have established what those foundational truths are. Conflict in the home often results from growing children challenging moral guidelines of parents. What you may interpret as hostility may simply be their misunder-standing of your valued beliefs or a basic disagreement with your worldview.

Your child will determine what he thinks you really believe, from watching the way you live. Give yourself time and space to decide why you live as you do. And then go on to construct your home firmly on that foundation.

• Within marriage, sexual fulfillment is natural and attainable. Even if you were a victim of incest or some other critical sexual violation, this doesn't give you license to live under the shadow of that memory. Don't bury the myth of romantic love. Love is hard to come by for it involves the pursuit of giving and sharing, kindness and patience, faithfulness and thoughtfulness, commitment and romance. Long-term sexual fulfillment is a holy ritual of marriage which builds both sexually and emotionally, nurtured by integrity and kindness.

Within this understanding of marriage, the pursuit of sexual well-being is essential. I don't just want to live with a kind, considerate woman. If I did, I could hire a housemaid. I've chosen to live with a woman who is capable and who cares about life. Sometimes this creates conflict. Regardless, she is the person to whom I give and from whom I receive sexual intimacy. This is important not only for our relationship, but because it establishes in our children's minds what marriage is all about. They watch us grow. They see us resolve tension. They feel our care and consideration for each other.

• Open your mind to the ambitions and dreams of your mate. The relentless social shake-up over the past two decades has done much to realign the old ways of thinking. Women are motivated toward careers other than being mothers or homemakers. They feel more prepared for the marketplace than they do for staying at home.

Family crisis occurs when men are threatened by these ambitions. A young woman may be less tolerant in putting up with an unhappy state than was her mother. Also, her economic independence gives her the freedom to walk away from the marriage. Men need to understand that a reordering of family duties is essential. Nurture of the children is not just the responsibility of the mother and neither is meal preparation. Talk through your ambitions and the daily needs of your family and decide together how you will order your household for the benefit of all.

- Your marriage needs to grow. The woman I married 20 years ago is different than the one I live with today. We grew up. Our likes and interests changed and became more finely tuned. I've been asked the question, "If you could relive your life, would you marry the same person?" The question is irrelevant, because over the years of marriage, we've both changed. We can't go back. Today as we continue to grow, we blend our individual needs. Thus we are able to stay married, not just because of our vows, but because we want to.

- Raising kids isn't easy. Problems occur in the most perfect of families. Some parents live under guilt inflicted by a misunderstanding of verses like, "Train up a child in the way he should go; even when he is old he will not depart from it." (Proverbs 22:6) A free Jewish rendition of the verse is, "Develop the gifts of a child when he is young, and when he is older he will be successful."

4
Hooked
on the Tube

The Media in general, and TV in particular, are incomparably the greatest single influence in our society today. This influence, in my opinion, is largely exerted irresponsibly, arbitrarily, and without reference to any moral or intellectual, still less spiritual guidelines whatsoever (Malcolm Muggeridge, *Christ and the Media*, Eerdmans).

The average five-year-old spends 65 percent of his time in front of the TV. When he graduates from high school, he will have watched from 15,000 to 22,000 hours of TV. He will have been exposed to 35,000 commercials and seen 18,000 killings. Television so dominates our world that engineers in large metropolitan centers are forced to redesign their water systems to accommodate the pressure change brought on by high water use during commercials ("What TV Does to Kids," *Newsweek*, February 21, 1979).

Television is synthetic, a fabricated composition of reality. Even the news finds its way to an editor who fits together the segments according to his plan and the time allowed.

Television is selective in that it shows the world according to the writer, cameraman, and editor.

Television is contrived. News documentaries, which we assume accurately depict real life, can easily be angled to suit the audience or wishes of the producer. This angle is often narrow.

In this synthetic, selective, and contrived view of reality, a child perceives the world, explores meanings, and accumulates a repertoire of images.

Futurists project ways that the television set will be used. People will simply hook up a keyboard to a set at home and do their work there rather than fighting rush hour traffic to the office. Mother will be able to do her family shopping by feeding an order into a computer attached to the TV set. Television will be used as an information center, as increased numbers of channels cater to different interest groups.

With the proliferation of channels and increased pay TV, there will be even greater attraction to TV watching. What is a Christian response to technology? Obviously, there is need for balance to recognize the good. But there is even greater need to insist that man master his technology. And this leads us to the real questions: How does television affect a child's development? What impact does television have on family and society?

As a medium of communication, TV mediates life for the viewer. It combines script, picture, and sound, carefully written and edited, to surround the viewer with a wall of thought. Ideas are both spoken and shown. Circumstances are so carefully contrived that viewer fantasy is cut off. Life is completely described, leaving no room for creative imagery or self-devised patterns. The implication is that this is how life is, with nothing to be added.

The paralyzing outcome is that the viewer is increasingly removed from either touching a friend or reflecting on reality. During the inordinate volume of time consumed watching TV, the child is not playing, touching, feeling, or experiencing the primary elements of life.

Primary experience not only brings the child in touch with life but also builds an ability to sort out, discriminate, and make personal judgments. Television works against this ability as it feeds the judgments and preferences of the producers and sponsors.

TV Affects Brain Functions

The most feared impact of TV is on brain and language functions. TV is primarily a visual activity employing little language. A one-hour documentary contains a minimum of words. The movement of action catches the viewer's attention before the words do. The show must first maintain interest by entertaining. A secondary goal is to affect behavior. An increase of rational thought is not usually an intention. As a medium of communication, TV majors on image and, thus, is nonpropositional and nonlinguistically centered.

Dr. J. Bishop, professor of education at the University of Alberta, has said:

> Because television must capture the viewer quickly and sustain his interest through the next commercial, the activation of the lower system is used most often. The heavy bombardment of colorfully intensive visual displays may be preventing children from forming well-developed receptors capable of sensitive and competent exchanges ("Children, TV, Play, and Our Responsibility," unpublished paper).

Studies demonstrate that TV promotes the production of alpha waves which tend to induce a relaxed state usually connected to semiconsciousness or daydreaming. Time gets lost and the mind becomes hazy. Parents complain that while children are absorbed with watching, it is hard to gain their attention. The rapid flow of images, color, and sound prevent them from easily returning to the real world. Pediatrician Dr. B. Brazelton describes this phenomenon as a trance.

"Just like an operating room light, television creates an environment that assaults and overwhelms the child; he can respond to it only by bringing into play his shut-down mechanism, and thus becomes more passive. . . . As they sat in front of a television set that was blasting away . . . they were hooked" (quoted by Marie Winn, *The Plug-In Drug,* Viking, p. 14).

Addiction is a word Miss Winn uses to describe the narcotic effect TV has on the viewer. TV induces a craving which never seems to be satisfied. She quotes a college instructor: "When the set is on, I cannot ignore it. I can't turn it off. I feel sapped, will-less, enervated. As I reach out to turn off the set, the strength goes out of my arms. So I sit there for hours and hours" (*The Plug-In Drug,* p. 21).

The duties and responsibilities of teenagers or parents are set aside. TV completely grabs hold, lifting us from the mundane into a never-never land as we watch the drama and excitement of the plot or game. The suspense holds us until the end and then it seems the commercial glues our eyes until the next show. This "hooked" effect leads us to underestimate its control. As with drugs, we believe that at any time we can shake off its control and go on with life. Adults may be able to shake it off, but children and teenagers caught in its web go from one hour to the next, from one show to the next, caught in the spell.

TV Affects Language Functions
We think in words. Language is essential not only to the larger cultural issues of a people but also for personal growth, for the development of ideas, for extending research, for perceiving

and defining reality, and for the arranging of a moral code. How does TV affect the growth of learning and language among our youth? Marie Winn points out eight vital issues:

• Concentration. Reading requires focus on material whereas TV, by visual and auditory stimuli, has greater brain control.

• Pace. The viewer has no control over the movement of the ideas or the story. Reading speed depends on the time the reader allows for reflection, absorption, and review. The power of TV is that there is no time to integrate the ideas into a cognitive process. If one thinks while watching, there is the danger of loosing the thread of the story.

• Peripheral vision. In real life our eyes see a broad vision or panorama. In TV, we are focused on a narrow picture which blocks out the peripheral world. This serves to "heighten our attention to the television image" so that we become glued.

• Rudiments of thought. The technology of TV makes it seem almost magical. The average viewer is not able to understand how it has been put together. When reading, a child can understand how the words are written and joined into sentences. It's something he is learning to do. "He takes on a far more powerless and ignorant role in front of the television set than in front of a book."

• Lazy readers. TV reduces the ability to absorb. Reading demands focus which tends to enhance the ability to absorb and retain. "The mental diffuseness demanded by the television experience may cause children who have logged thousands of hours in front of the set to enter the reading world more superficially, more impatiently, more vaguely" (*The Plug-In Drug,* p. 59).

• Post card culture. There seems to be a move among adolescents toward nonbooks like the *Guinness Book of Records* and the comics, toward material which is not a sustained narrative, which contains visuals with occasional words and requires little concentration.

● **Writing skills.** Universities express their frustration with an increasing student population lacking proficiency in writing coherent sentences. Some accuse primary and secondary curriculum, but it may be more accurate to consider the verbal skills learned by a generation raised on television.

● **Passivity.** TV as a highly technical device creates an environment which essentially entertains. Reading pushes a person out beyond the text to review personal meaning, while TV "leaves him unchanged in a human sense. For while television viewing provides diversion, reading allows and supports growth" (*The Plug-In Drug*, p. 64).

TV Affects Socialization

The family room has come to mean the place where the television is! The blue haze of the screen casts its hue over the room as the family settles down to argue about what show to watch. Notice the furniture arrangement. The seats are angled to the set, not to each other. And so for the next few hours one voice is heard. Occasionally someone may say, "Will you please shut up so I can hear the show!"

Television intensifies withdrawal from interpersonal interaction just at a time when a growing child most needs the interaction. A profusion of technology surely will not teach the skills of getting along with people. And so as the child bumbles along in the corridors of growing up, the environment of learning is shut off as the TV is turned on.

The Screen Actors Guild published a 10-year study of TV dramas focusing on what was represented as American. The stereotypes they found:

● Men outnumbered women three to one.
● Most women were under 30 and attractive.
● The few women over 30 weren't attractive.
● Older men were funny.
● Children comprised two percent of the population.

- Young men ran the world.
- Women weren't very bright and lived for romance, marriage, and family.
- Over half the population was between 25 and 45.
- Most people were white professionals, such as doctors, lawyers, and government officials (G. Gerbner and N. Signorelli, "Women and Minorities in Television, 1969-1978," Annenberg School of Communications, Philadelphia, October 1979).

By its presence TV is assumed to be a window on the world. And it does bring news and information from around the world into our homes. Yet by its programming, it constructs plots which serve its salability to sponsors based on potential viewer audience. Out of this comes an unconscious statement of what our world is really like.

Dr. J. Bishop gives his analysis:

> On TV sexual stereotypes abound with women who are often scheming, frivolous, and more often brainless than witful. Career women are cast in a neurotic light and youth is idealized beyond measure. Family life moves from crisis to crisis with fathers basically incompetent, controlled entirely by either scheming women or their own limited cache of sensible options. . . . Women are less law-abiding than men, even heroines are portrayed as deviant from community values ("Children, TV, Play, and Our Responsibility").

As a one-way visual medium, television denies the opportunity for a response transaction. As you sit and watch, you just sit and watch. The show is based on certain idealogical presuppositions. No time is allowed to stop the show and reflect on personal ideas.

Complex issues in TV programming quickly flow into resolution. The producer has a limited amount of time to tell the story and then wrap it up. Out of this time restriction comes a formula for success which aims at short-term goals rather than long-term ideals. Given the current views on success, resolution of conflict is usually realized by social status, possessions, self-indulgence, or good feelings. This quick resolution sucks the viewer into an emotionally charged drama. While he may shed a few tears, the viewer may be drawn away from solving his own crisis, vicariously living through someone else's dilemma. The success of the program's problem resolution may give mediated and temporary emotional resolution, while the viewer fails to be part of his own real life dilemma.

> Like the sorcerer of old, the television set casts its magic spell, freezing speech and action, turning the living into silent statues so long as the enchantment lasts. The primary danger of the television screen lies not so much in the behavior it produces— although there is danger there—as in the behavior it prevents: The talks, the games, the family festivities and arguments through which much of the child's learning takes place and through which his character is formed. Turning on the television set can turn off the process that transforms children into people" (Kevin Perrotta, "Watching While Life Goes By," *Christianity Today,* April 18, 1980).

The Effect of TV Violence

Does violence on television affect behavior? Some would argue no. But the unbelievable rise in crime and violence among our youth naturally leads one to ponder the influence of violence depicted on TV. If a high school graduate has witnessed 18,000 killings on the tube, isn't it fair to assume that there is some causal relationship between TV dramas and real life? A 14-year-old boy was shot by a friend in Sandwich, Massachusetts as they played with a gun while watching the slow-motion replay of the attempted assassination of President Reagan.

John Hinckley, Jr., who attempted Reagan's assassination, admitted that he closely identified with Travis Bickly, the cabby in *Taxi Driver* who had plotted to murder a political candidate.

Recognizing the trap of generalizing from particular stories, we best turn to social scientists. Leonard Eron, University of Illinois psychologist, and his associates have studied the level of aggression in society and the socialization of children. Their studies cover 25 years of research—875 eight-year-olds from Hudson River Valley of New York in 1960, a reinterviewing of 427 of the original subjects in 1970, and a three-year longitudinal study begun in 1980 among 600 youth in a suburban Chicago school district, including 150 from two inner city schools. Their findings are most convincing.

• Aggression can be learned from interaction in the environment.

• The less nurturing the parent is at home, the more aggressive the child is at school.

• The less the child identifies with both parents, the more aggressive the child is at school.

• The violent shows an eight-year-old preferred predicted his aggressive behavior at 19.

• There is a causal effect from violence viewing to aggressive behavior.

• There is a relationship between the violence a child watches and his behavior as a later adolescent, whereas the violence a late teenager views has little effect on his behavior. This seems to show that violence has a cumulative effect on the younger child.

• A youngster who is continually bombarded with violence on television may well come to think that aggressive behavior is the typical and appropriate way to solve life's problems.

• Girls are increasingly less likely to be influenced by aggressive television models as they progress through the primary grades, while the influence on boys becomes stronger.

• Three-year-olds are highly susceptible to violence.

• The more a person rehearses an incident, the more likely

he is to remember it and therefore to use it in problem-solving. ("Prescription for Reduction of Aggression," March 1980, and "Parent-Child Interaction," *American Psychologist,* February 1982).

Children watching violence during prime time TV tend to view the world as dangerous, possibly because a parent's presence reinforces the supposed reality of the program. Violence on newscasts can be more critical than on a show. The news doesn't show either resolution or consequences of violence— the aggressor is not punished. Although we have much yet to learn about violence as it affects children and behavior, we are already reaping the harvest from young minds sown with the seed of vicious, wanton acts of simulated aggression.

TV and Christian Values

Television is essentially designed to deliver a message and to sell a product. The 24 commercials per hour are the real framework of programming, since a show must fit that structure. Because a child in his first 20 years will watch one million commercials, it is important to ask what these commercials do. Professor N. Postman of the Department of Media Ecology, N.Y. University, suggests they teach that all problems are solvable. They are solvable quickly. They are solvable quickly by technology.

Themes surrounding the selling of a product usually appeal to basic human needs. Most recently, commercials are creating a warm, homey feeling, as if to suggest, "Aren't these companies wonderful? They let us buy their fine products." Television deals with only immediate problems, since it is essentially a "now" medium. The only measure of success is whether the program as bait, sustains an audience so the next commercial will hook the fish.

Recent pressure from parents for better programming almost begs the question. These parents recognize the negative effects that violence and materialistic values have in the shaping of young minds. Their protests have temporarily influenced advertisers to ask producers to create shows more in line with the wishes of parents.

But the haunting question remains: Is all this fuss about violence and values a way to alleviate guilt parents have for using TV as a baby-sitter? For one primary issue is the impact TV has in retarding the language and intellectual and social skills of the child. In light of this issue, withdrawal from television might be more to the point than "better" television.

Parents whose worldview is based on a world created by a God of justice, love, and truth need to question any communication medium which shapes the way people think. While you may hold to a Christian view of life, in the thousands of hours your child absorbs dramas, game shows, and cartoons, he sees a world devoid of God. Biblical themes and high ethical principles are either mocked or ignored. The powerful beliefs which have changed the landscape of history are flattened to rubble, and atheistic or amoral images are erected. This creates an illusion that Christian ideals and beliefs are irrelevant or stupid and that modern hedonism or humanism is all that exists or is worthy of commitment.

A person who really believes most of what TV proclaims or suggests would conclude that the cosmos is nothing but a freak accident of nature; and that man, set adrift, must make the best of it with no outside help. This powerful message shapes the view many people have of reality.

The counterbalance which Christian TV attempts to assert often comes across as an Elmer Gantry selling a god who is really a magician. After we watch the mutilation of thousands by starvation, war, or earthquake on the news, the next program features a testimonial by a celebrity lauding a God who helps him become rich or win a game. The lunacy of this type of religious magic serves to reinforce a banal view of God.

Television's stream of images tells us that man is creator. The fact of a God in control, demanding something of His creation, is simply ignored. Because of this, sin is also ignored, ridiculed, or simply discounted as a quirk of nature, a chemical imbalance, or an environmental maladaptation. The cosmic battle of sin and righteousness, good and evil, and of God and Satan are trivialized. The battle of good and evil is portrayed as one person against another, one being good and the other evil. The world is divided between the good guys and the bad guys. The biblical concept of a "good guy and a bad guy" struggling within us is ignored. It is so much easier in a plot to have one guy bad and the other good. The implicit message? That with all his problems, man is a good guy who will eventually triumph, given enough time, inventions, and power.

> Television . . . views the world without Christian coordinates. That media world of fact and fiction considers right and wrong in humanistic terms, never in terms of God's authority to set standards and to reward and punish. It defines freedom in material and political terms, rather than liberty from the dominion of sin and evil. In insists on knowing only the natural world, and on ignoring the supernatural (Kevin Perrotta, "Watching While Life Goes By").

Against this limited cosmic backdrop, the actors tell us that man and his world are gradually being improved. Missing is any knowledge of the New Testament drama of transformation. Yet when you eliminate the God of history, you effectively write off the possibility that a bad guy can by spiritual regeneration become a good guy. When a Charles Colson comes along, the inference is made that he grabbed on to a religious crutch. His spiritual transformation is regarded as a change in behavior to reinstate him in power and public favor.

For a Christian, the corroding effect of television is that by osmosis we will buy into the world's system. In his critique of TV, Malcolm Muggeridge says:

> I think that diversions are more difficult to deal with than ever before because the fantasies of life have been given such extraordinary outward and visible shape, even to the point where you can see them on the TV screen for three or four hours a day. These fantasies of power, of leisure, of carnality. Western men and women live in that world of images almost as long as any other, and it is a fearful thing. That is why you find among the young this extraordinary despair, because they feel there is no escape for them—no escape into reality. (Quoted by Kevin Perrotta, "Television's Mind-Boggling Nature." *Christianity Today,* May 17, 1982).

The endless flow of commercials, worldly heroes, movie stars, celebrities, and trends implicitly tells us that this world is really life and that beyond this, nothing worthwhile exists. The home is deluged with worldliness and because all this is viewed at home, a dangerous symbiosis develops. Because we watch television in the place where we feel secure and in control we receive it uncritically and tend to interpret the message from our desires for status, money, acceptance, power, and fulfillment. And it is easy for us not only to accept the values but to find ourselves nourished by what we see. The cumulative effect is this: without being conscious of it, we begin to believe what is shown and, consequently, question the fundamental value system expressed by Christ.

Compounding the problem is the amount of time we sit and watch, for not only does TV take us away from family and friends, but it takes us away from God. If the basis of faith is summed up in the commandment, "You shall love the Lord your God with all your heart, and with all your soul, and with all your mind" (Matthew 22:37), then how we spend our time demonstrates what we believe about God.

A parent's task is to help a child develop into an adult. This requires modeling and time. As parents we need to examine whether the way we spend our time and form our values is having a good effect on our children. TV is a numbing way to spend time. After dinner I sit down, sip a cup of hot tea, read the newspaper and flip TV channels. In an almost semiconscious state, I watch one program roll into the next, and before I realize it, the children have slipped off to bed, my wife is quietly crocheting, and the evening is over. What I watched is forgotten, and valuable time with children and wife is gone forever. Fun, dialogue, learning, reading, praying, going over the day's events and activities, the hearing of a victory or a loss, understanding the ways of God—all have sliden into lost time.

Many families are at the crossroads. There are fewer children to care for. Often both parents work and are tired in the evening and on the weekend. Because the parents are so occupied, the children feel bored.

One very easy out is more television. Technology is generating scores of new channels which will only serve to increase watching time.

It's time that we Christians get up, shut off the tube, and take hold of our lives. As Muggeridge said, "That is why you find among the young this extraordinary despair, because they feel there is no escape for them—no escape into reality."

5

A Place to Stand

Values are attitudes expressed in daily life. A father who ignores local charities and pours his income into things and pleasure expresses to his children this value: "I come first." A mother who takes time to read her child a book states this value: "You are important."

Values are structures of right and wrong, better and best. Values are how we believe, not what we believe. Values are the expression; truth is the substance. Values are the framework; truth is the foundation. Based on our views of truth, we express our values.

In years past, it was easy to assume that Americans and Canadians accepted certain values. We lived with the illusion that, because North America was Judeo-Christian in its founding, the ethics and values naturally flowing out of this religious tradition would continue to reinforce our structures and laws.

But today, in searching for tolerance, we have excluded religious considerations. The scientific age has produced a self-confidence in man which leads many to regard religious ideas as unbecoming or obsolete. With so much of the world in disarray, the conclusion seems to be that no one is in control. For many, secularism has replaced the Judeo-Christian foundation.

Secularism

Secularism is one way of viewing man and his world. Secularism excludes the transcendent and supernatural. Secular man may still accept religious worship, culture, symbolism, holidays, artifacts and even language, but he does not have a religious worldview,

> ... the view which sets all earthly issues within the context of the eternal, the view which relates all human problems—social, political, cultural—to the doctrinal foundations of the Christian faith, the view which sees all things here below in terms of God's supremacy and earth's transitoriness, in terms of heaven and hell" (Harry Blamires, *The Christian Mind,* Servant Books, p. 3).

The current debate on evolution/creation is an example of how our educational system has come to accept secularism as a fundamental means of interpreting our world. The biology teacher has just finished the opening lecture on the origin of man. His arguments rest on the assumption that out of millions of years of haphazard mutations, man came into existence.

Don raises his hand and asks the question, "Is there any outside force which controls or guides this process?"

The teacher replies, "We don't know. Either such a being does not exist or, if it does, we have no way of knowing it."

Two issues are at stake. First, the Christian worldview is assumed to be either irrelevant (it doesn't make any difference) or unknowable (there is no empirical means of knowing). Second, the process of creation or (how it happened) becomes the central point of the lesson. The control factor (who made it happen) is eliminated. The debate warms when the two sides, Christian and secular, argue over how it happened.

Christian concerns should not be focused on the process but on origin and control. As soon as procreationists debate evolution, and press for a biblical process explanation, they begin to lose the battle as they get caught in the field of scientific jargon, definitions, so-called facts and dating.

The real battle isn't in the details of "how." The question of evolution isn't a scientific problem resolved by the laboratory, but is a theological question. If there is no God, then the nature of man is simply as you find it. On the other hand, if there is a God who in His counsel created man, at this point setting aside the discussion on process, then man's nature has origin, definition and purpose.

Public education has assumed that the notion of God is unworthy of mention, and so secularism as a worldview has become the underlying assumption. Transcendence is either mocked or ignored.

The creationism debate illustrates the confusion in establishing values. If we move away from an all-knowing, caring Creator to an unknowable or nonexistent creator, this has a profound impact on the way we choose our values. Even if all sides arrive at an identical value (like being good to your neighbor), the logic of arriving at that value differs. If you begin with a knowing, caring Creator, you have a basis on which to affirm that loving your neighbor is important; it comes out of God's design. In creating man, God had a purpose.

Since values require a foundation, the real concern must be centered on where we begin. Pluralism (many foundations) eventually works its way out into how we live. The Christian adult who is concerned about the values of his children needs to carefully analyze the assumptions on which his own values are based. Otherwise, he may find himself accepting and even

perpetuating values which are really relics of former generations, or values which are non-Christian in origin.

Christian schools are an attempt by some parents to deal with
secularism in a pluralistic society. But church-related schools
don't automatically solve the problems of secularism. It is one
thing to have a Christian setting, with its culture and language. It
is quite another to think in a Christian way. The danger is that in
disclaiming secularism, considerations become limited, as
sectarians assume that only a few people (usually themselves)
are the recipients of truth. Their teaching may be nonsecular,
yet exclude much that is sacred.

If secularism is the rejection of transcendence, then to be
Christian is to live under and search out the fullness of the
transcendent. Sectarian religion tends to exclude much of
God's world because of its narrow traditions. In the intention of
serving Christian thought, it may deprive children of much of
God's world.

Secular humanism has become a whipping boy. Popular
usage tends to distort its meaning, necessitating a brief
definition. Used as an adjective, secular means: "Worldly affairs
or things not religious: not concerned with religion or churches." As a noun, humanism is a "system of thought or action
devoted to human interest and ideals." Linked together—within
the current debate—it means a view of life that excludes any
notion of God or a supreme being, and centers on man's
interests and abilities. We can best understand the strife about
secular humanism when we recognize the Judeo-Christian
ethos has been watered down by a host of new ideas and beliefs.
For example, the Moral Majority opposes the influence that
secular humanism has exerted. However, it may be more
accurate to say that what they oppose is the multiplication of
interest groups and ideologies which do not grow out of a
traditional God-centered explanation of life. But this is pluralism, not secularism.

Comfort

Within this growing complexity of value systems, who really influences a child? The answer is difficult to isolate because of our open, pluralistic society. A simplistic reaction would be to accuse the media alone. Magazines offer a wide variety of sexual come-ons. The flood of pornography is very powerful. Movies and television become ever more risqué in their scenes and messages. But these are symptoms rather than cause. Society expresses what it believes. The film industry produces what will be bought at the theater. A TV advertiser determines what people will watch. If sufficient numbers of people will watch the show, the advertiser expects a reasonable profit. Entertainment is ultimately based on what people want.

As the family life lessens its impact on value formation, the child is left to an ever-broadening variety of influences. The uncertainty over values in adult society obscures rules a growing child needs to learn and live by.

"Parents spend all their time trying to find out whether a child should be treated this way or that, but there is no effort to look around and say, 'Hey, what do we believe in? What do we want this child to believe in?' " So writes Dr. Robert Cole, Professor of Child Psychiatry at Harvard. He suggests that many parents are afraid to bring up children on their convictions and moral faith. They are intimidated by all they hear from the so-called "experts" and thus abdicate their religious or political higher vision.

Cole comments, "Having turned away from God, they are left with themselves—their own comforts." When he asks parents what they believe in, they often say, "In my children." Cole says, "Now when children have become a source of almost idolatrous faith, this is quite a burden for children to bear. Parents forget that what children need perhaps more than anything is discipline and a sense of commitment to something larger than themselves. Children need to be asked of as well as given to."

Self-Fulfillment

The most significant recent factor in reshaping our value system is the instinct for self-fulfillment, liberation, and the advancement of personal rights. Daniel Yankelovich proposes that the shaping of society emerged from man's search for self-fulfillment. In discussing the "me-first" mentality, he comments.

> As a grass-roots phenomenon, the quest for self-fulfillment is, inevitably, a creature of its times, borrowing its forms of expression from whatever sources are most convenient. Unfortunately, the materials closest to hand have been the odd combination of a psychology of affluence and an outlook whose tenets are: love for the moment, regard the self as a sacred object, be more self-assertive, express all feelings, hold nothing back" (New Rules, pp. 234-235).

This searching for values within the orbit of self-fulfillment also includes avoidance of ideas which are no longer necessary and, therefore, not worth the effort. Discomfort, self-denial, anguish, sorrow, difficulty, adversity, rigor, pressure, hardship, and affliction must be avoided at any cost. This reaction to trauma is based on the premise "that the human self can be wholly autonomous, solitary, contained and 'self-created'" (Yankelovich, *New Rules,* p. 237).

Sacrifice for others and even for self is scrapped. Long-term gains, if they involve sacrifice, are rejected. "Meaningful experience" has become an in-phrase. Lacking a fixed star, we seek experiences which will give meaning to our shrinking cosmos.

The human potential movement is a powerful current that focuses energy on the self. In his best-selling book, *Your Erroneous Zones,* Wayne Dyer writes, "You are the sum total of your choices." Bred with optimism, man can discount any value in spiritual answers, and look for answers inside of himself.

The self's potential will then be unlocked and one becomes free to discover the "real self." Wonderful things happen. One becomes spontaneous, autonomous, natural and creative. A fulfilled person gradually emerges from behind the blockage (Yankelovich, *New Rules,* p. 237).

Pleasure has become the measuring stick for values. The growing middle-class, with increased options of pleasure, has established fulfillment as its criteria. Exotic travel promises love-boat rituals. Boredom with paying mortgages and sustaining the self-interest of kids and spouses leads people to extramarital affairs. It seems that when the dying world is flashed on our screen, we like the priest and the Levite, quickly pass by on the other side. We demand employment with meaning and, of course, with a shorter working week and additional benefits. Food is more of a pastime than a necessity. Gourmet cooking has become the rage—if it isn't exotic foods, it's health foods or diet foods. We take to the roads and jog ourselves into shape; we load our bedside tables with the latest books on exercise, fat reduction and the ways to expand our inner potential.

Pleasure is inextricably linked to our value system. The dream once fixed in our minds becomes a right. We are in a hammerlock: we despise the inefficiencies and double-talk of government; yet if they dare remove benefits and securities, we petition, picket, and ultimately throw them out.

Yankelovich comments on this compulsion toward desire fulfillment:

> You are not the sum total of your desires. You do not consist of an aggregate of needs; and your inner growth is not a matter of fulfilling all your potential, needs, wants and desires; and by learning to assert them more freely, you do not become a freer, more spontaneous, more creative self; you become a narrower, more self-centered, more isolated one. You do not grow, you shrink" (*New Rules,* p. 242).

Our unreasonable expectations have seriously overburdened society. We all want the government to take less and deliver more. Senior citizens increase in number, while fewer working adults underwrite pension plans and security. We harangue the justice system for more and better protection. Incensed that prisons are not rehabilitating prisoners, we insist on tougher laws. Other peoples immigrate, often to do jobs our citizens refuse, and then we react negatively to the values they bring. The media oversaturate us with a plethora of trivia, hopeless diversions, and insane situation-comedies. Lawyers proliferate and bureaucracies shuffle under their inertia—all in the interest of the good life.

What Can You Do?

• Live what you believe. A parent cannot expect a child to pick up his values by osmosis. It takes personal nurture and care. A parent who walks away from church attendance because of disinterest, boredom, or anger, needs to carefully rethink his spiritual life. If you are a Christian attempting to grow in your faith, understand that a moral foundation needs building blocks.

When you were a child, what did you see in your mind when you thought of God? I saw a man 5'9", 190 pounds, and bald. He was my father, Hilmer Stiller. But for me as a young child to understand a transcendent God, I had to begin with someone I knew. I needed a reference point to God. We use human language and symbols to convey our understanding of who God is.

My children's interpretation of God the Father is a transfer from what they know of me as father. Awesome? Yes. And it means that my beliefs need to be more than a random selection of ideas.

One of the most beautiful references to father and child is in a story Jesus told. "If your boy asks for bread, do you give him a stone? If he asks for fish, do you give him a snake? If he asks for an egg do you give him a scorpion?" (See Luke 11:11-12.) I can't imagine a father giving his boy a stone that looks like a piece of bread and then delighting as his son crunches down on the stone, chipping his little teeth. How ludicrous. But the father not only needs to care; he must know the difference between bread and a stone. It's not enough to provide food. Do you know what's best? Have you tried and tested? Or do you send your children away, hoping someone, somewhere will do what you never had time or interest to do?

• Balance your beliefs with sensitivity. I remember walking into my parents' bedroom late one night. Sitting on the end of their bed, I asked, "What should I do with my life?" I was finishing high school and had considered three options—professional sports, law, or the ministry. We chatted about it and finally Dad said, "Brian, you are at the age when the choice must be yours." Timing, that's what it was. They were in step with my development.

Later I learned that they had prayed since I was a child that I would choose a vocation within the church. I never knew that. They never indicated that was their hope. They believed I would go in that direction, but gave me the freedom to grow and make choices without making me feel I would let them down if I decided on another pursuit.

Your relationship with your children should not be tied to their acceptance of your beliefs. Real beliefs are internalized—they come from within and influence life. If their beliefs are simply a restating of yours to maintain a bond, you only assist them in developing insincerity.

Remember the marvelous story of the son who was tired of living at home? Asking his father for his inheritance, he left home and within a short time was broke. He finally got a job feeding pigs. One day he thought, "Why, even Dad's hired men live better than this," and so he thumbed a ride home.

Celebration and happiness took over. He was given symbols of acceptance; a ring, shoes, fine clothes, and a banquet.

Notice how the father handled his beliefs and values:

—His son was of age and wanted to leave home. This conflicted with the father's desire, but the boy needed to make his own choices. So he let him go with his part of the inheritance.

—He waited for him to come home. When I make wrong choices, I know the heavenly Father is waiting. His acceptance is there just as soon as I recognize my failure.

—He didn't rummage in the past, but celebrated the future. Celebrate the future of your children. Be excited about their choices. (See Luke 5:11-32.)

• Distinguish between beliefs and values. A belief should be based on that which is true in all places and times, and for all people, on universal, transcendent truth. A value is based on time and circumstance, and is an application of what you believe. Values are the interpretation of beliefs within a particular setting or circumstance.

In the early church there was a dispute over eating meat that had been offered to idols. The belief was, "Be thoughtful of your Christian brother and avoid doing those things which will cause him uncertainty." The value was, "In this time and culture, don't eat meat offered to idols if it offends your brother." Being sensitive is good for all places and all times. But the business of the meat-eating was localized by time and space.

• Don't avoid punishment and discipline. Punishment? In our enlightened world? For too long we have lived by the notion of freedom and acceptance failing to design a balance.

Discipline is the exercise of restraint and conditioning to change and direct behavior. As the child grows, approval and disapproval help to shape his patterns. It is hoped that discipline will eventually produce self-restraint and appropriate action.

Punishment is a means of repaying the wrong and acknowledging the guilt. It is a way of saying that wrongdoing will not go unrecognized. It tells the wrongdoer that he has paid for his wrong and can go on living, without the load of guilt. The Bible recognizes the need for punishment. Our acceptance by the Father required that someone take the punishment for guilt. Jesus by His death took it. For a child, punishment (and I speak only of merciful punishment) should clearly identify the wrong. Its aim is not to change behavior—that's discipline—but rather to point out the reality of the wrong.

Actions have consequences. When you act a certain way, you encounter certain results. This fact points out the moral nature of life.

How shall our children learn mercy unless it is shown to them? How shall they learn that wrong deserves punishment unless they are not only disciplined, but punished? How shall we as parents accord our children the dignity of true humanity unless we teach them that their moral wrongs merit punishment and that punishment in some ways rights the wrong they have committed? How shall we teach them the sinfulness of sin if we treat it as a bad habit we can train them out of? Punishment may teach a child to quit sinning; but it should be given if it is truly merited, whether it will make the child quit or not (Dr. John White, *Parents in Pain,* InterVarsity, p. 199).

Go With Your Round Sides

As a parent you have strengths. In building values, don't be afraid to pass these on. They're a part of who you are. I have a friend who is one of the original entrepreneurs. He loves a challenge. His oldest son is following in his footsteps. Another friend is deeply concerned with the plight of others. His spare time is spent initiating social solutions. In watching his children and hearing their conversation, I can see the continuity from the parent to the children.

There are times I become a little anxious knowing there are flat sides to my life. But I must work with what I have and let the strengths of my life nourish my children.

Someone has said, "Give me a fulcrum, a place to stand, and a lever and I'll move the world." We do need a defined value system to order our lives and our society. But order is not the status quo. Order allows creative change.

And nowhere is this more true than in Christian experience, as we follow Christ, led by His Spirit, into the ever-newness of life that He promises. . . .

You have taken off your old self with its practices and have put on the new self, which is being renewed in knowledge in the image of its Creator (Colossians 3:9-10, NIV).

If we are living this way, we can teach our children how to.

6

Games
Without Rules

I watched the two families. They were embarrassed, angry, and confused. "It can't be true. Not our kids," the parents said. Karen's father was pastor of the small community church and Lorne's father was a deacon. Just the night before, Lorne had gone to both parents to tell them of Karen's pregnancy. They were both seniors in high school.

How did two such nice kids get caught? Both came from respectable homes. As I sat with the families, I heard their questions of anger, saw their self-recrimination and embarrassment. They finally decided that Karen and Lorne should get married. For them, it seemed the only "Christian" thing to do. I pled with Lorne's father not to force marriage, but for him there was no other option.

The marriage lasted about a year. Today Karen and Lorne are married to other partners.

Many parents make two false assumptions about teenagers and sex. The first is that today's sexual preoccupation, liberal attitudes, and explicit description of sex have transmitted useful information to our youth. Many parents I talk with assume their

71

teenagers are well informed. They conclude that with all the sex magazines sprouting up, there is little more they can say.

Parents also assume that their kids not only understand how sex works but what sex means. But intercourse is not all there is to say about sex. Our kids have been sold a false bill of goods. They haven't been told that sex takes a lifetime to understand; that it's not what you do but what you are; that it's intrinsic to all of life.

That day with their parents, Lorne and Karen wept out of confusion. Many adults are confused too. Some press for more education on birth control, while others advocate more available abortions as a means of preventing the situation that Lorne and Karen found themselves in. Both solutions are short-sighted, for they fail to deal with the issue of sexuality.

Much later, Lorne told me, "It's taken me six years to quit hurting. Why didn't someone tell us how foolish we were to get married?"

Sex Education

"Brian, have you seen the book recommended for sex education in our school district?" my wife asked. I hadn't. And I wasn't too concerned either, but agreed to take a look at this controversial book. We walked into the bookstore and settled our children in their reading corner. Lily led me to a table surrounded by young teenagers, nervously giggling, flipping the book from page to page. Attempting to look casual and disinterested, I wedged my way in and picked up a copy.

My first thought was that it was a book for those getting married, or for those who needed counseling on sex techniques. I was wrong. The photographs were of nude boys and girls in their early teens.

This claimed to be a book on sex education. It was really a book of photographs showing positions for intercourse and other means of sexual stimulation.

My reaction was anger at the author's distortion of the meaning of sexuality. To them sex is mechanical. Lost is the understanding of the psychological and spiritual realities that blend with the physical into oneness. The writers exploited sex to sell a book. Under the guise of "education," a respected publisher got into the act. A school board's decision to use this material clearly demonstrated their fragmented view of sexuality.

"If the devil can't change the love, he changes the definition," commented Jay Kesler. With all our supposed complexities and sophistications, love is still often reduced to physical experience. Not surprisingly, the culture reinforces the notion that if it feels good and doesn't hurt anyone, it's OK. Lost is the understanding that love is giving, not getting.

"Virginity is about as useful as your appendix," commented a U.S. psychiatrist and author. She claims she is against intercourse for kids who are 15, but considers it acceptable for 16-year-olds. Her Camp Discovery, located on Cape Breton, Nova Scotia, is accredited by the Canadian Camping Association. Discussion about sexuality is promoted and the camp has no rules against sexual relations.

An article titled "What Should We Teach Our Kids About Sex?" listed a series of questions teenagers should ask themselves:

- Am I physically mature?
- Am I well informed about birth control and can I discuss it with my partner?
- Do I care deeply about this person?
- Do both of us want this to happen?
- Will intercourse occur in a place where I feel safe and comfortable?
- Do I feel free of guilt, fear, a need to deceive anyone important to me?
- If, in spite of all precautions pregnancy occurs, am I

prepared to cope with that? (Fredelle Maynard, *Chatelaine*, September 1980).

Conspicuously absent are any questions of morality. The premise is—if it makes you feel good and there is no guilt, discomfort, or resulting inconvenience, then it's OK. Sexuality in this context has no more significance than a sports activity or social experience. A nurse and supervisor of community workers with Toronto Family Planning Services commented, "I have no trouble with young people—even 14-year-olds—having sex, so long as it is for the right reasons." But is there ever a right reason for a 14-year-old?

Teenage sex is occurring at ever younger ages. A Guelph University study found that out of 486 Ontario teenagers visiting birth control clinics, 34 percent had had sexual intercourse by the time they were 15. Other studies show that 53 percent of teens between the ages of 15 and 19 have had intercourse. In North America, thousands of teenage pregnancies occur each week. The average age of these young parents is 16!

There is increased opportunity for young people to discuss and learn about sex. Clinics are springing up across our land. Schools are offering courses that present detailed sexual information and allow for questions of the most explicit nature.

Given this open forum for discussion, why are so many kids getting in trouble? There are two contributing factors. First, puberty occurs earlier than it used to. It is estimated that menstruation begins six months earlier each generation. One hundred years ago only 13 percent of women would have been considered fertile by 16 years. Now that figure has jumped to 94 percent.

Second, the average age of marriage among women has risen from 18 years to 22 years. With the physical maturation lower, and the average age of getting married higher, a longer period of time exists in which a teenager, fully adult in body, experiences sexual tension. This brings enormous pressure on the teenager to sublimate the tension, to masturbate, or to have sexual encounters.

Two studies demonstrate the extent of teenage sexual activity. UCLA psychiatrist Aaron Hass learned that among 15- and 16-year-olds, 43 percent of boys and 31 percent of girls have experienced intercourse. In Saskatchewan, a primarily rural community in western Canada, a government report showed that 35 percent of the 15- to 17-year-olds and 61 percent of 18- to 19-year-olds have had intercourse. The average age for the first occurrence was 15 years and 7 months. Over half said they had frequently dated that partner before; 31 percent said it was a casual acquaintance; and 8 percent said they planned to marry that person (Aaron Hass, *Teenage Sexuality*, Macmillan, 1980).

Teenage Pressures
Apart from the early physical development of teenagers, there are a number of factors which relate to this radical change in sexual activity. Understanding these pressures may help adults think through the appropriate measures that need to be taken.

● Inner confusion. An adolescent growing up is naturally confused by physical changes. For a girl, this can be especially traumatic. Her sense of identity is often affirmed or denied by how she thinks men perceive her. Added to this, her menstrual cycle is a constant reinforcement of the power and mystery of her body. To further complicate her dilemma, it is usually the girl who is forced to assume the role of saying, "That's far enough" or of accepting responsibility for pregnancy, should that occur. If the girl's mother was repressed or molested during childhood, she may be conveying overt or subliminal messages to the daughter which will only add to her anxiety. Her inner confusion may be expressed by giving in to the surrounding pressures.

For a growing boy, the realization of his role is complicated by his sexual desires. Wet dreams and the urge to masturbate serve to further stimulate his newly discovered sexual appetites. The surrounding culture constantly reinforces a virile male image, and provides stimulation to his sex glands by pictures, symbols, and blatant nudity. For most boys, information about changes taking place in their bodies is not supplied by fathers but by "the boys."

• Coitus fetish. The heavy message among many teenagers is that if you aren't doing it, you aren't making it. Teen sex has been exploited by the movie industry. Intercourse has become an obsession, beginning in the adult world and eventually filtering down to youth. Orgasm is a dominant theme of many adult movies, books, and TV programs.

• Search for self-esteem. To be liked is to be wanted. To be wanted is to be accepted. To be accepted is to be of worth. Self-esteem is slowly built up as the teenager attaches personal interpretation to experiences and relationships.

The fragile self-image of an adolescent is often close to collapsing. The trauma of the acceptance/rejection tension can be severe enough to cause a nervous breakdown. A teenager with low self-esteem may give sexual privileges to entice or reward. For a girl, it is the old story of "giving sex to get love." A boy's search for self-esteem may take another route. In order to have stories to tell to "the boys," he may become more aggressive. He wants to overcome personal fears and to more actively seek out girls who measure up to the requirements of his male peers. For a boy, it may be the old story of "giving love to get sex."

• Depression. Usually considered an adult problem, depression has become a significant problem among youth. The pressures of life generated by family, friends, failure and future can induce depression.

Contradictory as it may sound, a teen's permissive behavior may be employed as an unconscious warning signal. Entering into sexual relationships may be a call for help or for attention.

• Aggressiveness. Adolescents who are unsure of themselves often express their insecurities by aggressiveness. Boys caught in delinquency are usually in trouble because of some physical aggression against society or another person. Girls, on the other hand, usually express their aggressiveness by shoplifting, running away from home, truancy, or sexual promiscuity.

• Repression. Some teens have less interest in sexual activity than do their peers. This may simply be due to later maturation or preoccupation in other activities. But for some it could indicate a deeper disturbance. In a girl, sexual repression may take the form of: *compulsive energy*—putting all her efforts into school work, hobbies or sports and giving no time to building interpersonal skills; *obesity*—making herself so unattractive that the possibilities of sexual interest are eliminated; *anorexia nervosa*—starving herself even to the point of death, to avoid social roles. If a girl is repelled by her own sexuality, she can by starving remove a basic part of her sexuality, since menstruation will probably cease.

• Feelings. "Things are changing so fast these days, the important thing is to give kids a sense of self-worth and integrity so that they will act responsibly in a relationship." This was the comment of a child psychiatrist, as he fielded questions from parents at a PTA meeting. Like many, he regards responsible action as something which occurs when you have a feeling of self-worth.

But feelings of self-worth don't necessarily lead to responsible sexual behavior. Our world has become so preoccupied with "good" feelings that "bad" feelings have been interpreted as evil and "good" feelings as nice.

Teenagers face a rush of conflicting feelings. To use feelings as a criterion for choosing appropriate action just doesn't work. A teen is so vulnerable to his own feelings and to those of his group that he simply lacks ability to adequately discriminate

between the networks of feelings. Also, his hormonal maturation and physical growth have much to do with his rapid swirl of
inner feelings.

An adult's preoccupation with feelings presupposes sexual
maturity. To superimpose this yardstick on an adolescent as a
measurement for good and bad is not only naive but dangerous.

• Sex education. On Phil Donahue's show, two women
debated the pros and cons of a local clinic providing information on sex to teenagers. The clinic's representative was most
persuasive as she told stories of teenage girls, unable to talk with
their parents, who came to her for help. Her opponent, a
representative from United Parents, overreacted as she awkwardly explained the disruption the clinic caused to family life.
Finally a member of the audience asked the clinic representative, "If a 13-year-old girl came to your clinic asking where to get
an abortion, would you give her the information and agree not
to inform her parents?" Her affirmative response was greeted
with enthusiasm by the audience.

Since many teenagers have little communication with their
parents about sex, if they get into trouble they receive little
assistance from their parents. They do need somewhere to go
for help. But the question still remains: Should a government-
funded agency, with no accountability to the parents, provide
sensitive information on sex to children? To do so has moral
overtones and denies parental involvement in life-changing
decisions.

A parent who doesn't care about sexual choices his child
makes may think this type of help is acceptable. But what about
a parent who believes that his religious and moral views are
worth transmitting? Should a local agency, funded by public
money, provide information on abortion, contraception and
sexual behavior, without the parent's knowledge or consent? A
counselor at a local clinic commented, "If parents are so

concerned about pregnancy, why don't they teach their children alternate means of easing sexual tensions?" This again illustrates a mechanical attitude toward sexuality, and ignores the value questions that need to be raised.

• Female consciousness. Many people have assumed that sex means something different to women than to men—that women seek for intimacy while men seek for gratification. This stereotype has been resisted by the women's movement.

The male/female image change is not without reaction. Women increasingly refuse to be labeled as homemakers. Their desire to move in a broader circle has generated a backlash among men because it is threatening to the male ego.

The male/female conflict produces an absence of a clear sex role for a child to emulate. A woman may get so caught up in proving her newfound freedom that the rest of the family must serve her in this new pursuit. If her husband has been raised with defined roles of man/woman, he may not be able to make the transition quickly enough. In this war, the child walks alone in a no-man's-land.

• Pleasure. Shorter work weeks, more disposable income, greater opportunities for recreation, travel, and hobbies help make the pleasure wheel go around. Much of adult society has been geared toward fulfillment and enjoyment. In examining the effect of this pursuit, social scientist Daniel Yankelovich comments: "On traditional demands for material well-being, seekers of self-fulfillment now impose new demands for intangibles—creativity, leisure, autonomy, pleasure, participation, community, adventure, vitality, stimulation, tender loving care" (*New Rules*, Random House, p. 14).

In the new cult of sex, pleasure has been made the high priest. The adult consumption of sexual aids and techniques and adult preoccupation with "love boat" affairs inevitably affect the youth world. As adults define the meaning and fulfillment of pleasure, youth will seek for pleasure—whether the context is vocation, recreation, or sex.

● Separation. When the pill hit the market, a sexual revolution began. First it allowed sex and procreation to be separated. Procreation was for the birth of a child, sex was for pleasure. Second, sex and marriage could be separated. Marriage no longer called for having babies and raising a family, and one didn't need to marry to enjoy the pleasure of sex. This shift has changed the traditional patterns of marriage and sexual activity, and the young person is the heir of these values.

● Abortion. "We gear our surgical and committee system toward abortion as early as possible. Prompt abortion has every advantage—it's safe, quick and inexpensive," commented Dr. P. Gillette of Montreal's General Hospital.

Abortion isn't so much a life-saving device for the mother as a new form of contraception. Why the phenomenal increase in abortion? In an insatiable drive for pleasure and personal convenience, many people have turned to this medical procedure to rid themselves of inconveniences called children. The impact on young people? A clear signal that whatever restricts their pursuit of personal peace and prosperity can be pushed aside without reference to moral or ethical questions. The message has been heard: "If unborn babies cramp your lifestyle, flush them out."

● Homosexuality. Mike sat chewing a piece of bubble gum. His lanky body tried to hide his embarrassment for the tears dripping slowly off his face. He was a good-looking kid of 17, and he needed someone to listen. His father, a respected leader in the community, was unaware of Mike's problem. Listening took time because Mike's feelings were so confused. For years they had been building up. Now, untangling the web required some gentle persuasion.

"Brian, at first I didn't know what it was. When I finally knew I was attracted to boys, I felt so rotten. I hoped it was just a problem of masturbation, but it was more than that."

Mike was president of his church youth group and played trumpet in the school orchestra. He got along well with his parents and two sisters. But the more he became involved in extracurricular activities, the further he retreated into himself. Yet everyone thought he was OK because he was doing well.

"There was no one I could talk with. Dad never really told me about sex. In fact, he almost seemed pleased that I didn't chase the girls. And so I've tried to push it out of my mind.

"Do you know what this means, Brian? It means I'm queer!" His shoulders began to heave as the silent tears turned to convulsing sobs. Years of submerged anxiety and guilt flowed.

Homosexuals have kept stride with the rights movement. Radical demonstrations and clever manipulations of the media have served to deliver their message loud and clear. Their all-pervasive claim of legitimacy and normalcy has worked its way into our social fabric.

Many young men and women struggle in a tug-of-war between what their feelings tell them, and what they hear from society, on the one hand, and the rejection they experience in churches, on the other.

Science has not been able to tell us the exact source of homosexual inclination. Theories are conflicting. Some say it stems from the genetic structure. Others say it is a result of environmental conditioning. However, we do know that it is in conflict with God's design and that such practice is forbidden in the Scriptures.

Those who accept the biblical standard need to have concern for how the church deals with this problem. Usually, there is no opportunity for a young person to be heard without condemnation. The strident judgment by churchmen against gay movements tends to eliminate any chance for a young man like Mike to be heard. For Mike, speaking meant he would be heard. And to be heard would mean judgment and rejection. And so he had turned his cries inward.

• Pornography. *The Toronto Star* reported: "It was your typical pornographic movie—lovers acting out a fit of sexual passion. . . . There was no artistic merit, no redeeming social value. With one exception, the porno stars were said to be between 10 and 12. They look younger. The lights snap on in the screening room of the Ontario Police Headquarters." The film gave police all the evidence they needed to press charges against the film's producers.

Across North America, this industry reaches into billions of dollars. With a higher demand for "kiddie porn," adults pay inflated figures to see children engage in sex. With the introduction of home video centers, the ability to make and see such tapes will push the industry to unbelievable porportions.

Who are these people? In our community, two men were recently convicted. One was a 57-year-old engineer who had sex with his 11-year-old daughter while his wife took the pictures. The other was a 30-year-old librarian who induced young boys to perform indecent acts while he took thousands of pictures. The Man-Boy Loves Association, The Pedophile Liberation Organization (PLO), The Pedophile Information Exchange (PIE), and the 10,000-member Childhood Sexuality Circle which advocates sexual child-swapping, are just some of the organizations advocating sex with children.

What Does a Parent Do?

A parent's job is to guide children into adulthood and independence, and there is no way to avoid walking through the mine field of sexual development. As you guide them in how and where to walk, you hope to lead them to maturity and happiness. The following principles may help.

• Be a good example. Don't mystify sex: let your kids know you and your spouse are in love and that sex is a natural—and private—expression of your lives. They should recognize that home and marriage is the place for sex. Kids will be secure when they know Mom and Dad are in love.

• Understand their pressures. When I was a boy, the see-through blouse provided a daring exposure of female anatomy. Today, magazines are splashed with nudity and are available at the corner newsstand.

The young person lives in a world guaranteed to produce confusion—flagrant exhibitionism in the media, growing sexual self-consciousness, physical changes, peer pressures, and questions about values. Try to see the world from where a teenager stands.

• Be honest. Find a suitable time and place to talk to your children about sex. Even in our open world, when it comes to talking about sex, we seem to lose our nerve. Don't rely on sex education from school or chatter from the back alley. Regardless of your discomfort, it is best coming from you. Keep the discussion impersonal, and don't use it as a time to pry. The fact that you care enough to discuss it is an opener that allows them the opportunity to come back. They'll quickly learn whether or not the subject is taboo.

• Realize that active glands have no conscience. There are some situations in which a teen cannot be trusted. For example, a girl and guy in a home alone are made vulnerable to their own glands. A simple rule should be—no staying in a house where there are just you two, even for a short period of time. Building trust with young people does not mean putting them in settings which push their natural inclinations beyond control.

• Agree with your spouse on limits and curfews. Make sure your children understand the limits. The process of setting limits is itself helpful to their maturation, and may be the very thing which will help them keep out of trouble. Don't be sucked in by the plea that everybody is doing it. On the other hand, don't be insensitive to what other families allow.

• Distinguish between lust and love. This distinction is vitally important to your teenager and will help him to be responsible about sex. His inner urges and his desires to express affection tend to get confused. The sex drive is always loud enough for him to hear. But the containment of this urge is difficult to hear in our permissive society. Again it becomes a matter of example—what they see in their parents.

• Teach personal self-discipline. Maturity is defined as the ability to postpone gratification. Once a young person begins to be promiscuous, he will keep moving in that direction. As he understands the value of holding back, it will not only generate a sense of personal discipline, but will keep him off the treadmill of having to gratify every felt need.

• Teach God's design. Your children should often be reminded that they are made in the image of God, that they are His workmanship (Ephesians 2:10). They need to know that their bodies are part of God's creation and intended for wholesomeness and purity.

Your children need to be taught biblical attitudes toward their own sexuality, as well as toward marriage and family. Otherwise, their main source of information about these crucial subjects will be from a secular world which, at best, disregards the Christian view and, at worst, completely contradicts it.

Don't be threatened if you are conservative by nature. Just because others are glib and open doesn't mean you are old-fashioned. Frankly, we have made too much of sex as a recreation and too little of it as God's means of intimacy and purity in marriage.

Your children need to be directed. As you guide their lives, recognize that you will make an occasional mistake. That's OK. As you are learning to be a more effective parent, God is alongside you, helping, coaching, calming, and correcting.

7

Trapped in the Jungle

It's the strong who survive in the jungle. Yet kids who live in the concrete jungles may look very alive but really be growing up partly dead. Two factors that contribute to this slow death— delinquency and drugs.

Delinquency

Three 12-year-old children, two boys and a girl, work as a team. While the two boys kick a soccer ball in the yard, Wendy picks the locks and works her way into the house. Within a few minutes she finds $10 in cash and $1,000 in jewelry. She leaves the house and with her team moves to another street. Why do they steal at this young age? Because they need money to pay for their costly drug and alcohol habits. If they're caught, the overloaded courts have no adequate place to send them. And the probation officer's case load is just too large. So they get lost in the bureaucracy (C. O'Neil, *Toronto Star*, March 21, 1981).

It used to be that younger girls committing crimes stayed with truancy and shoplifting, and left the rougher play to boys. Recently that's been changing. Lucia appeared in court 27 times for breaking and entering, theft, assault, causing bodily harm, and robbery. Her home is in a middle-class Canadian suburb where she lives with her alcoholic mother and two sisters.

She remembers attacking other children when she was 10. At 12 she started having sexual intercourse and began with drugs, drinking, and tried her hand at shoplifting. When she was 14 Lucia stabbed another girl.

The demographics of Canadian cities are quite different than those of large U.S. cities. Canada does not have the traditional city ghetto with high unemployment and slums because provincial and city governments tend to build subsidized housing projects in the suburbs. Thus, those on welfare are mixed with middle-class communities. However, in Canada as well as in the U.S., children and teenagers are committing an ever growing number of crimes.

Psychiatrist Russell Fleming concluded that half of the young people involved in crime live with only one parent. One third have a history of violence in their own families ("Our Violent Society," *Toronto Star,* January 5, 1980).

For some teenager criminals, home is in a fashionable neighborhood. Like John. At 15, he is experienced at breaking and entering. For two years he has lifted thousands of dollars in cash and jewelry from houses.

Why are these kids turning to crime? For many it's an answer to boredom, frustration, and confusion. At times they see nothing better to do than to smash a window or beat someone up. Nurtured on the TV image of affluence, they assume that another person's property is theirs also. Believing money is all-important, they quit school and then discover that their limited skills and experience aren't enough to get a job. Because the cost of living is much higher than they expected, the desired freedom is less accessible. In frustration, they become part of the largest unemployed group in North America—singles under 25.

Today's justice system is preoccupied with the offender and has little interest in restitution for the offended. Probation exercises modest control. Where large training institutions exist, increased criminal skills are picked up by the delinquent. Residential group homes provide a more acceptable form of retraining under a controlled environment, but at great financial cost.

Remember the good old days when misbehavior at school meant dipping Susie's pigtails in the inkwell or shooting a spitball at Harry? Well, those days seem to be gone. For so long the educational system followed the theory that new forms of education would save us from racism, poverty, greed, and social chaos. This gave way to experimental forms and more permissive attitudes within the school system. Parents viewed educators as knowing more than they did and expected the schools to do the job. Little did they know then what dreadful changes would result.

Here are some examples of the problem:

- In 1980, the cost of vandalism in Canada was $50 million.
- In the U.S., 40 percent of robberies and 36 percent of assaults on urban youth took place on high school campuses.
- A $2 million fire was ignited by student arsonists in the beautiful northern Ontario community of North Bay. In a high school of 1,500, nine students committed suicide last year.
- In 1978, 100 murders were committed by school children in the U.S. There were 12,000 armed robberies, 9,000 rapes and 204,000 aggravated assaults against teachers, 270,000 burglaries and $600 million in school property damage.
- The U.S. National Institute of Education reported that each month 282,000 junior and senior high students were attacked and 112,000 were robbed. Some educators say the figures reported are only 10 percent of the actual number.
- A 13-year-old student killed a teacher with a semiautomatic rifle. His father was a former White House press

secretary (Toba Korenblum, "The Hostile Halls of Learning." *Macleans,* May 26, 1980 and Connie Cronley, "Black Board Jungle," TWA *Ambassador,* June 1978).

What are the real reasons for the problem? Can we afford the luxury of saying, "It's the school's fault" thus sweeping responsibility from our doorstep?

The educational system is obviously a reflection of a society. It may be ahead or behind in its philosophies and methodologies, but society eventually forces the system to express its own values.

Because our society is pluralistic, there is no one ethos, even though the initial constitutions and laws were based on Judeo-Christian thought and heritage. We have many recent immigrants whose cultures have little in common with our own. And yet it has not been these, but people whose roots come from Judeo-Christian soil who have revolted against their heritage.

Educational needs and styles have changed as schools attempt to update their teachers in educational philosophy and methods. For example, when I was in school, the good student had the right answers. Today, because computers are much more competent than people at storing information, the good student has the right questions.

School tensions are aggravated by the radical social change which has swept our communities. Kids bring the angry hurt, fear, and anxiety of tension-filled homes, to the halls and classrooms of our schools. For six hours a day, their collective phobias, aspirations, hurts and energies mix in a boiling caldron of educational distress. Toba Korenblum puts it succinctly:

At the heart of the vandalism-violence controversy is a long-standing pedagogical debate. Should schools be expected to cope with the emotional well-being of their students as well as intellectual? Many educators just throw up their hands in the face of social and economic conditions—family breakdown, drugs, child abuse, declining school enrollment, cutbacks and youth employment ("The Hostile Halls of Learning").

Teacher and author Peter McLaren writes, "Vandalism reflects the disease of our society, a society that doesn't have much to offer kids to express their dignity and self-worth" (*Cries from the Corridor,* Methuen Publishing House, 1980).

William H. McGuire, President of the National Education Association, a 1.8 million member U.S. teachers association, commented on authority in an interview:

Virtually all institutions are being questioned by the public. Schools, of course, are not immune. They have been the subject of the same criticism and lack of trust. And students who are raised in this environment pick up on this. The genesis of it all is frustration ... at school ... with life and society. It can find expression in lighting a fire in a waste basket or stealing expensive equipment from the classroom.... Any ill that society discovers it now turns over to the schools. In addition to teaching students to read, write and do arithmetic computations, there have been increasing pressures to meet other needs—driver training, family education, vocational guidance, life adjustment, drug education, needs of the handicapped. The burden of filling out forms and other paperwork falls on the classroom teacher ("Classroom Violence, Public Apathy," *People* Magazine, September 1979).

Developmental psychologist James W. Prescott, sees a link between absence of physical affection toward children and their later inclination to apathy and violence. He believes that violence indicates brain damage and that this damage occurs in the early days of childhood, coming from a lack of touching and loving by the parent. Thus the deprived infant may lack impulse control and later become violent. Prescott concludes:

The possible lesson for modern countries is clear. We seem to be suffering from breakdowns in affectional bonds—reflected in everything from rate of divorce to sexual crimes, alcoholism and drug abuse. Culture is the handmaiden of our neurobiology and without a proper environment for physical affection in a peaceful harmonious society, it may not be possible" (*Psychology Today*, December 1979).

We have added to the work load of our schools. Teachers aren't only to convey information and develop skills. Now they must also maintain law and order and develop survival techniques. What can a teacher do when potheads take over the classroom? Or when kids who are afraid to use the washrooms suffer physical discomfort all day?

The constant flow of children, out of control, walking the streets, is a reminder that they have never been controlled. Believing that children will naturally find an adequate personal ethic and morality is nonsense. They build their lives out of watching us build ours. As adults we are responsible for what they build. We must work alongside, giving guidance and encouragement when they grow weary.

This assumes several controls:

● A strong home setting, where Mom and Dad provide a place of security and stability.

● An acceptance of their individualism without giving them license to do what they want. Respect who they are and encourage them to become all they choose to be.

● Established guidelines. Be reasonable, but agree with the parents of their friends about boundaries of behavior, time, friends, and freedom. Children need the exercise of having to live within the fences. Let them learn to be obedient.

● At the danger of invading their privacy, insist you know where they are going, with whom, and what they are doing. Guard your children from their own instincts and maturity until you know they can handle situations. Given too much freedom, a teenager will inevitably get into trouble. A high percentage of teenagers who engage in sexual activities do so in their parents' homes. Leave kids alone and you encourage sexual activities.

Drugs

Dolly Gallant was only 14 years old. For over a year she had been sniffing contact cement and glue. Sitting by her boyfriend, she took a plastic bag, sprayed it with Pam and began to sniff. Within two hours she was dead. Her lungs had collapsed. The combination of soybean fat and Freon II was deadly.

Sniffing produces a powerful, almost instantaneous rush, more powerful than any other form of induced high. A sniffer who starts with one tube of airplane glue eventually needs 10 or 12 tubes to get the same sensation.

A young girl said, "It feels like you're floating. Sounds get louder and softer, lights get brighter and darker—the good part of your childhood comes back to you. You want it and want it."

Each day thousands of North American kids, some as young as seven, sit around pouring contact cement, nail polish remover, and lighter fluid into a tissue, or dumping airplane glue into plastic bags or Pam cooking oil into containers, all in the simple preamble to sniffing.

Talk to adults about drugs among youth and they see long-haired discontents happily sucking on a marijuana joint, or prostitutes crying out for a heroin fix. Seldom do they hear or see children and teenagers riding a merry-go-round in the drug-induced fantasy world.

For Dolly, the components of the cooking oil destroyed the grease in the lining of her lungs. She was a victim of a product marketed for the family kitchen.

Tony began at seven. He stole from his father's wallet and bought what he wanted. Five years later he learned about bootlegging drugs, selling LSD, hashish and grass. His last year in school was grade 7. He left home and traveled. Today Tony is

20 and looks old.

Kim is 15 and in grade 10. She looks like an average, clean-cut kid during school hours. But she has skipped classes to make a "connection." She is buying hash oil from a 17-year-old boy who goes to another school. For two years she has used drugs and is terrified at the thought of her parents finding out.

Frank was 12 when he had his first trip on airplane glue. He would stay out until 2 or 3 in the morning and his mother seemed to have no control. He was put in various homes, but to no avail. After attempting suicide by slashing his wrists, he returned home. Today Frank is 19, jobless, dating a girl who is addicted to glue. He has tried to quit but can't. A mother of a glue addict said, "When he got high once ... he tried to crawl into my arms like he was a five-year-old again. He cried and whimpered and said, 'O Mommy, I love.' He was so pitiful, my son, my son" (Liane Heller, *Toronto Star,* October 13, 1980).

Andy is 13. He hangs out with his friends, smokes grass and hash, and wants to try LSD. He has a "friend" in grade 9 who has introduced him to drugs. He takes his movie money and smokes every weekend and sometimes after school. As Andy says, "All the kids at school say grass is better than cigarettes and won't rot your lungs."

Drugs, both legal and illegal, continue to warp, distort, and destroy. Kids with little or no parental control may end up in court. But many from solid homes gradually destroy their bodies and minds, not facing a judge or jury, but simply wasting away in mindless trips.

In Toronto the estimate is that one in four students from grades 7 to 13 smoke marijuana at least once a year. The dilemma for some is whether we make an occasional smoker into a criminal or whether we decriminalize the offense and put it under the Food & Drug Act. This would make it more like a traffic violation, with a modest fine.

Part of the underlying momentum for this change has come

from the popular usage of marijuana since the hippie culture of the mid 1960s. This view suggests that cannabis (marijuana) is quite harmless and less destructive than tobacco or alcohol. But in response to this, recent studies show alarming evidence of the damage inflicted on users of marijuana. The most threatening of these effects are in the brain and reproductive systems. Marijuana has high affinity for fatty tissue and since the brain and the sex organs are high in fatty tissue, it tends to concentrate itself in these areas. A recent study on marijuana reported:

> Cannabinoids—more than 60 chemicals found only in the cannabis plant, whose dried leaves yield marijuana—are highly soluble in fat. Unlike alcohol, which is water soluble and therefore works out of the body in a relatively short time, cannabinoids take weeks to be gradually eliminated. They accumulate in vital organs—most significantly in the brain, testes, and ovaries. Those considered most susceptible are users whose organs are still developing—children, from unborn babies to adolescents. And almost all pot smokers are teenagers and young people in their childbearing years (Janice Tyrwhitt, "Marijuana Alert I, Brain and Sex Damage," *Reader's Digest,* June 1980).

In the past the strength of marijuana was relatively low, 5 percent of Delta-9-THC, the mind-altering component. Now it has been discovered in some cases that it has risen up to 5.5 percent. Dr. Alexander Jakubovic, a biochemist at the University of British Columbia, commented that the old beer-strength marijuana is now whiskey strength.

By using electrodes, changes have been discovered in the limbic system which is directly involved in control of sex drives, appetites, and emotions. Dr. R. Heath, Chairman of the Department of Neurology and Psychiatry at Tulane Medical School, New Orleans, investigated the effects of marijuana on monkeys. "It would seem from the monkey studies that you have to smoke marijuana for only a relatively short time, three to four months in monkeys, in moderate to heavy amounts before evidence of brain damage develops."

The sexual organs are clearly affected. For males marijuana reduces the production of testosterone. Dr. Robert Kalodny of the Martus and Johnson Institute of St. Louis, reported that men 18 to 30 years of age who smoked pot for six or seven years experienced a significant drop in sexual activity. Dr. Wylie Hembree, of Columbia University College of Physicians and Surgeons, showed that one month of heavy smoking resulted in:

- lowered sperm count
- decrease in sperm mobility
- increase in abnormally shaped sperm.

In women it suppresses hormones which control the function of the ovary and a decrease in prolactin, a hormone essential in the production of milk.

Marijuana has been shown to have the following effects on childbirth:

- A higher chance of losing a baby during pregnancy, at birth, or shortly after birth
- Subtle developmental abnormalities in the offspring's tissues and organs
- Lack of infant maturity
- Potential decrease in the size of reproductive organs in offspring
- Retardation in growth and development
- Nervous system abnormalities, with a high-pitched, catlike cry from some newly born
- May inhibit the formation of DNA, the genetic material that orchestrates cell functioning and division (Janice Tyrwhitt, "Marijuana Alert I").

Dr. Frederick W. Lundell, Senior Psychiatrist and Director of the Adolescent Clinic at the Montreal General Hospital, gave the following illustrations:

A 17-year-old girl, pretty and popular from a middle-class home, was caught forging checks and pawning her mother's ring. Her parents had not realized that her falling grades and arrest had any connection. For five years she had been smoking pot with her friends and had gotten so seriously in debt to pushers that she resorted to stealing to pay for her habit.

A male teenager was afraid he was homosexual because he had not experienced the changes that normally go along with puberty. The doctor, realizing that marijuana can suppress the hormone that develops secondary sex characteristics, confronted the young man with his use of pot and initiated an endocrine treatment.

Ian, a 15-year-old patient, had been smoking pot for four years. He had been dropped from both a private and public school. Psychological testing showed a discrepancy between his natural and current ability. For example, he failed simple memory tests and couldn't recognize a coin, button, or paper clip by feeling them with his eyes closed ("Marijuana Alert II, Enemy of Youth," *Reader's Digest,* November 1980).

Dr. Lundell followed through on 100 cases and discovered that teenagers who smoked marijuana lost their desire for life, purpose, and ability to reason. "Some dropped out of schools, jobs and sports; others sat through classes like vegetables." One 15-year-old boy, with above average intelligence, would have a joint in the morning. His morning notes were below average and the afternoon notes were meaningless scribbles. Another boy of 16, finished high school before his friends. By the age of 20 he was beyond psychiatric help and by 24, was wandering the streets following a religious guru.

Those who wish to legalize marijuana should keep in mind that there is a causal relation between drugs and crime. If marijuana is legalized, its production will increase. Marijuana is both habit-inducing and harmful to the body. For example, four marijuana cigarettes per week produce lung damage equivalent to 16 regular cigarettes a day! And we see increasingly how the brain, sex organs, and nervous system are damaged.

Many drug users view life as something over which they have no control. Their self-confidence is low and tends to be greatly influenced by peer values. Yet they withdraw from intimate relationships and allow drugs to further distort their misguided attempts to be adult before their time.

Alcoholism

As we sat down to lunch, Gordon quickly blurted out, "Last night Graham (his 17-year-old son) came home drunk. The police picked him up at the hockey arena. At first I was scared ... police cruiser, reports and all that. But we were so relieved to learn it was just booze and not drugs."

Often parents are more relaxed when their kids get drunk than when they use drugs, simply because the parents are more familiar with alcohol. This naive response to alcoholism is a tragic commentary on the maturity of adults. For alcohol isn't passive, nor does it produce happy memories. Rather it distorts the mind, eats away at the family, and washes lives up on the rocky shoals of failure. The slick advertising of the liquor industry is a lie. Behind the happy faces and attractive copy are these real facts.

- In the U.S., 8,000 teenagers are killed each year in alcohol-related traffic accidents. About 40,000 are injured in traffic accidents.
- There are 3.3 million problem teenage drinkers, and of these 1.3 million are considered serious.

● Close to five percent of the teenage population is alcoholic. It is startling to note although the legally defined level of intoxication is .10, over half of teenagers involved in traffic accidents have blood concentrations of .02, the usual level after taking one drink. This shows that the normal level used to determine intoxication may not be accurate in dealing with youth.

These statistics don't begin to describe the human tragedy. For some children whose parents drink, it literally means little or no food; Dad has spent the grocery money. Others fear taking their friends home, unsure of the state of their parents. The liquor advertisements never tell us of teens whose lives are messed up, either because they have become victims of alcohol or because their parents are wrapped in liquid chains. Never do liquor companies film a young person angry or frustrated, unable to cope with the pressures of homework, because he is living between the 'dry' and 'drunk' periods of a confused parent.

Out of the homes of America walk teenagers whose values, lifestyles and dreams have been crushed by the senseless babblings and incoherent values of parents captured by alcohol.

We protest againt the liberalizing of drug laws and quite rightly so. Yet as we protest, governments rake in hundreds of milions of dollars on tax revenues from the sale of alcohol. Yes, we have learned from the 1930s that prohibition only stampedes the black market, involves the underworld, and doesn't bring a solution. Nevertheless, the vast profits made by growers, producers, and marketing groups are often gained at the expense of young people whose lives slowly erode as their minds, bodies and relationships get caught up in the unending game. In our protest over the freeing of drug usage, let's not forget that alcohol, a sea of despair, is also laying siege to our youth.

8
Dead on Arrival

Both teenagers look so happy. I carry their pictures in my Bible. When I open it I see them and remember. Today Michael and Jennette are dead, not from some cancerous disease, but by their own hands. Their bodies are silently decaying in a Quebec cemetery. Their voices will never again ring out. Michael died first. Five months later, Jennette followed.

There was no one to listen to the bitterness and sorrow of Michael's failure in school or the beatings Jennette received from her father. Not even a priest to say the last rites. The evening news said nothing about their deaths. A few arrived for the funerals and stood awkwardly at the graveside.

We didn't hear their cry. They were cut off—isolated from parents and friends, left with only their impulsive reactions to a very stressful situation. Their sense of powerlessness triggered that last desperate attempt to regain power, but in so doing, the remaining vestige of life they controlled was snuffed out. In grabbing for control, it slipped through their fingers. The cry quickly faded away. No one had heard the build-up of silent sounds as life departed. No one was there to hear the last rasp of the throat.

At 12, Jeff was a big boy for his age. He seemed to be cheerful, always joking. One morning, after his mother had left for work he took an 18-foot extension cord, a friend's ladder, climbed a tree behind the apartment building, and hung himself. In anguish, his parents asked, "Why did he do it?" Although both parents worked, his mom didn't like being away from home. She had suggested to Jeff that she stop working so they could do more things together. Jeff knew that meant they would have to live with less. "Why should we live without things?" he asked. The only note he left was scrawled on the back of a math test— "This is it. Last day. Good-bye forever."

John's teacher told him he was a sensitive, creative student and that he had high potential. But John thought of himself as an absolute failure, because his high school marks were consistently low. His friends said he always managed to mess up just when things seemed to be going well. The psychiatrist called it a classic case of adolescent angst, an intense feeling of guilt. Just before his final exams, John drove into a friend's garage, shut the door, and left the engine running, waiting for the carbon monoxide to do its work.

John had tried to end his life twice before by jumping from a bridge and then in slashing his wrists. After his death, John's parents found a series of notes. One was a check written for the sum of "Endless Amounts." Another said, "I've finally completed something I've always wanted to do. I remove the guilt from each person. . . . P.S. Happy Father's Day."

Teenage Suicide

Teenage suicide with its mysteries and fears remains locked behind closed doors, a reality almost beyond our ability to face. There is a lingering hope that adolescence still is a time of innocence and joy. But teenage deaths boggle our minds. We look enviously on the opportunities of the young, and ask: "With the world at their doorstep, why do they back away, closing the door forever?"

Suicide ranks as the second largest teenage killer in North America, outnumbered only by car accidents. In the U.S., 1,871 teenagers between the ages of 15 and 19 killed themselves in 1979. Among white males 15 to 24 years of age the rate doubled from 6.6 per 100,000 in 1950 to 13.9 per 100,000 in 1970. Among nonwhite males it jumped from 5.3 to 11.3 per 100,000 during the same period. In Canada there was a 400 percent increase in teenage suicide from 1965 to 1980. (Elizabeth McAnarney, M.D., "Adolescent and Young Adult Suicide in the U.S. a Reflection of Societal Unrest?" *Adolescence,* Vol. 14, No. 56, Winter 1979, p. 765).

Teenage suicide occurs in a variety of ways—drug overdose, shooting, hanging, jumping from buildings or bridges, slashing of wrists, deliberate car accidents, and jumping in front of moving cars or subway trains. More bizarre methods include swallowing sharp objects or volatile liquids. These suicides usually occur between 3 P.M. and midnight, and most often during the spring and summer. Females will attempt it three times more than males, though males are four times more successful. Many of these boys are above average in intelligence.

Most suicides are attempted within earshot of the parents. Young people who live in troubled families where there are problems like alcoholism, previous suicide attempts, or divorce are much more prone than those who come from stable homes.

Young people contemplating suicide view death in a variety of ways. A child may see it as magical. An adolescent, closer to being an adult, will see it as less magical and more of a no-win situation. For some kids, suicide is a cry for help, or a way of seeking attention, with no real intention of dying. However Dr. Barry Garfunkel, a Canadian authority, after observing 505 attempters concluded, "For the most part, these kids wanted to die."

Causes
Because of the current wave of suicides, researchers are attempting to identify the causes.

• One theory suggests it is a result of chemical deficiency. Many psychiatrists are connecting suicide to childhood depression.

• Two hundred young people who called into a crisis intervention center, and were later treated in an emergency medical facility for attempted suicides, were used as data for a study. It was discovered that of the 200 suicide attempters:
— 26 percent were male and 74 percent were female.
— White teens were rated high on alienation and non-whites were rated low.
— 63 percent were between 16 to 18 years. 65 percent lived with only one or neither of their natural parents.
— 33 percent had experienced a broken romance.
— Conflict with parents and lack of communication were significant contributors (F. Wenz, *Adolescence,* Vol. XIV, No. 53, Spring 1979, pp. 19-30).

• Young people who had attempted suicide were asked to list, in order of importance, the crises operative in the decision to attempt suicide. These were: social conflict with peers, conflict with parents, broken romance, economic status of parents, communication problems with parents, school performance, step-parents, and a broken home.

• Dr. Elizabeth McAnarney, in her studies among 15- to 24-year-olds, compared U.S. youth with those from Japan, Sweden and Scotland. She makes the following observations.

In societies where family ties are close, suicidal rates are low. About 45 percent of those who attempted were from broken homes. A stable marital situation lessens the likelihood. Loss of the intact family, whether by death of a parent, divorce, or separation becomes an important variable.

In cultures where the majority belong to a formal religion, suicides are low. Where there is no formal religion, the suicide rate tends to be high.

Groups in transition have higher rates of suicides than stable ones. Young people of the inner city, immigrants, and people frequently transferred are frightened, missing the stable family or religious affiliation, and see suicide as an alternative.

Young people from families who highly value achievement, feel heavy pressure exerted to succeed, and may choose to take their own lives rather than fail.

Suicide is aggression turned inward. In cultures where agressive feelings are suppressed, suicides increase. When aggression is openly expressed, suicide rates are lower.

Adolescents quickly learn the limits of aggression. They view violence on television, but are taught that society punishes such behavior. When they get angry, they don't know what to do. Rather than get in trouble with parents, they internalize their feelings. Inward aggression and self-destruction may seem like the only solution to a teenager who is upset with school, peer pressure, and family disruption ("Adolescent and Young Adult Suicide in the U.S.).

A surprising observation was made by Kenny in his study of 28 teenagers who attempted suicide because they refused to risk the consequences of expressing outward hostility. These 12 girls and 16 boys were compared to 21 other adolescents, similar in age, race and socio/economic background, who had not attempted suicide. The suicide attempters showed a high level of visual/motor problems similar to those of children diagnosed as learning disabled. They had also failed more grades in school and had a history of suspension, truancy and other behavioral problems (T. Kenny et al, "Visual Motor

Problems of Adolescents Who Attempt Suicide," *Perceptual and Motor Skills,* Vol. 48, 1979, pp. 559-602).
• Family disorganization and its impact on suicide was studied by Dr. F. Wenz. He called the lack of norms or morals that govern conduct as normlessness, and the sense that the family lacks power to cope as powerlessness. He concluded:

> The greater the normlessness—lack of norms, values and role definitions—the greater the potential for suicide.
> A person who attempts suicide may do so out of a sense of powerlessness—the family's inability to cope. This feeling may rise because a family whose norms and values are weak, and even contradictory, gives the young person a sense of helplessness.
> The suicide attempt is a last effort toward restoring some sense of personal power.
> Suicidal behavior may be an extreme reaction to family disorganization. A teen's only form of escape is to adopt some type of retreatist behavior (*Adolescence,* Spring 1979, pp. 19-30).

• Chicago psychiatrist Dr. H. Visotsky states, "To some extent, the epidemic of adolescent suicides can be traced back to Vietnam. Young people became disillusioned with the magic of government and this extended to all institutions, including the family." He gives an insight into suicidal rates among the well-to-do. The competition ethic leaves the affluent child feeling even more alone, making it more likely that he will take it out on himself, rather than on society ("Suicide Belt," *Time,* September 1980).

Whatever anger poor people experience is usually acted out in antisocial ways such as vandalism, homicide, and rioting. The sense of shared misery in the lower groups prevents people from feeling so isolated.
• Following his study of a high suicide incidence among

young people in Chicago's affluent North Shore suburbs, Dr. A. Tobin concluded there are three kinds of adolescents who could become high suicide risks. First is the delinquent type boy who, in failing to live up to the expectations of his parents, gets into trouble by driving wildly and generally being a nuisance. Second is the perfect child, most often a girl, who is very unhappy with her parents' standards, but generally never shows it. Third are the drug users and anorexics or self-starvers who are outwardly angry ("Teenage Suicide and Affluence," *Sources and Resources,* August 15, 1980).

It is not surprising that kids cave in. One international crisis follows another. Social change closely follows the erosion of traditional values. Because of their immaturity and sensitivity, young people are the first to recoil from the shock waves. Acting as shock troops in our society, they are the first to feel the waves as they come up over the hill. And they are unprepared to face the enemy.

Preventing Suicide

Most parents don't ask about suicide until someone close to them makes an attempt or dies. Then they want to know: "How can I help to prevent such a tragedy in my family?" Three areas deserve attention.

● Suicide threats. Most children fantasize about death, especially following rejection or punishment: "They'll wish they had treated me better when they see me lying dead on the road." As the child gets older, and if the sense of rejection is increased, fantasy may be worked out in real life. Since suicide is often an attempt to gain recognition or a call for help, one must try not to overreact but to look behind the event to the causes. Don't be manipulated by threats of suicide; but when they happen, stop and listen.

● Adolescent change. Changes in behavior are part of growing up. Research is showing that there are particular times when the personality can undergo radical change in just a few months. Thus, it is important to watch for these five signals:

—A total withdrawal from peer activities. Most teenagers at some point experience rejection by peers. Their reaction may be to withdraw. If the withdrawal becomes total and sustained, it is necessary to talk through the problem.

—Loss of sleep and extreme fatigue. Stress will hit a teenager when he is least prepared. Young people face interior issues and experience severe emotional pressures as adults do. This may result in sleeplessness. If fatigue continues, some stressful situation may trigger a negative impulse that will lead to suicide.

—Self-disparaging remarks. Many factors lead a child to conclude he is insignificant, in the way, or useless. If self-esteem is eroding, lack of parental affirmation may reinforce the child's latest desire to bow out. We all need to be counted worthy by someone.

—Decline in schoolwork. Motivation to achieve is often missing in those who decide to end life. One barometer of this may be the sharp drop-off in school attendance. Other factors may contribute to a lack of interest in school, but when you see the drop-off occur, search for the cause.

—Giving away of possessions. This may be a conscious or unconscious signal that the child wants to be remembered after he is gone. For some, suicide is the final act of personal control and power, and giving away prized possessions can very well be the preamble.

● Poor grades don't mean low intelligence. A child who learns more slowly than his peers is often shunted into a slow learners class. The problem may, in fact, be a learning disfunction, such as slow motor development, dyslexia, or a neurological problem. The learning disability may cause the child to conclude that he is stupid. School, parents and peers often reinforce this estimate. Personal confusion may work its way out in aggression or through increased withdrawal at home and school.

Need for Permanent Relationships
The radical change in family patterns constitutes a seige against our children. The high divorce rate may mean that a young person is neglected or pulled into a whirlpool of antagonism. An empty house after school, with no one to hear, "Hi Mom, I'm home," may add to his feeling of detachment.

In some homes the atmosphere is so catastrophic that young people really can't deal with it. Hostility toward parents with no hope of resolving the conflicts may reverse into personal destructiveness.

An adolescent is on the road to adulthood. In a stable setting, a teenager may pass through this period without major problems. A teen learns from an adult model. If this model is removed, a vacuum is created, and the young person may resort to impulsive, self-destructive behavior to avoid confronting his personal inadequacies all alone. He needs strong ties with parents that are permanent and continuous, for his identity to be secure. Two primary ingredients for healthy growth are a continuing adult model and enough time together to weave the fabric of relationships.

Need for Christian Faith
Christianity is not magic. Problems don't disappear with one application. Religious experience can easily become ritualistic —a ceremony to observe, or legalistic—a law to obey. A growing child may become bored with ritual or aggravated by legalism. Parents need to recognize the child's spiritual dimension and nurture the formation of personal values and beliefs.

Some teens find little reason for hope in the circumstances of their lives. Christian faith helps a teenager see beyond the negative situations and relationships. Christian hope is not an emotional fantasy separate from reality but is rooted in historical fact. God came to us in a form we could understand—the man Jesus who entered into life and was observed in history. His life, words, and accomplishments were observable. He was flesh and blood. Life wasn't lived in abstractions. As a boy working in His father's carpenter shop, real blood flowed from His hand when the chisel slipped. He talked about truth in the language of His people. His words were not superficial. He got to the core of life. He brought real cures to inner sicknesses.

Because of God's self-revelation, especially in Jesus, Christians believe that life has a beginning and an unending future. Life is not an endless repetition of lives. Nor does it end at death, for life is going some place. Creation finds its beginning in God. Man, made in God's image, has significance.

God wants to call me "friend," and seeks me out so that a relationship can be established. He goes out of His way to keep me within the orbit of His love. But He allows me to choose for or against Him. I'm given the freedom to live within hearing distance of His voice, or walk off alone.

Because man abused and disrupted God's intent for Creation, God stepped in and provided a means of resolution. Jesus Christ paid the debt of my bankruptcy and the penalty of my wickedness. He wills to restore Creation to its original purpose and give freedom to man. That is where history will find its resolution, within an eternal time and place.

Such a view of life and of history gives me a sense of purpose. I am made in the image of the Creator. I have meaning. There is rationality to life, a sense of ultimacy that gives direction to my life. My place in eternity is determined by my choices. There is a hell to shun and a heaven to gain.

What does this have to do with suicide? Everything. Man is restless until he has found meaning and purpose. The growing malaise of hopelessness corrodes the mind. Even for one who doesn't consider suicide, the endlessness of working, mowing the lawn, cooking meals, leads to the question, "What is life all about?" Men and women at midlife wonder about significance. We all want to write our signatures on the universe. If in my death, my life is seen to have been of little consequence, then why live? Even more tragically, if death is seen as the end, then the pain of life has no meaning. For a Christian, all that happens has significance.

As adults, we need to carefully examine why we approach life the way we do. Whether we are conscious of it or not, we all live from our way of seeing life. The pessimism and despair plaguing adults today is a direct expression of a worldview. Our day-to-day lives answer the questions: Where do we come from? How did we arrive? Where are we going? Who is in control?

Young people are greatly affected by the presuppositions of the adults who influence their lives. It's hard to expect teenagers, just shedding the skin of childhood, to rise above the pressures that adults lay on them. Perhaps the most significant way is to provide them a solid foundation of faith which anchors life into the truth and presence of our God, and which is lived out by the adults most dear to the young people.

9
Playground of Despair

Lately I've been in gynecology and obstetrics. It is absolutely frightening to see what's going on. The wards and private rooms are filled with young girls. ... Their insides are torn to pieces. It is impossible to describe the repair jobs we do. These girls suffer from every kind of sexual abuse. It used to be that doctors treated prostitutes in such condition; now we have to treat girls from the best of families. ... Every day we see girls in their teens with disease and infection (Florence Rush, M.D., *The Best Kept Secret: Sexual Abuse of Children,* Prentice Hall, p. 2).

Family violence is a two-pronged problem—incest and child and spouse abuse. Incest and child and wife abuse are emerging social diseases which mirror our society.

Incest
Katherine Brady was only eight when her father, a prison guard, soothed her fears during a thunderstorm by taking her into his bed. Her mother worked as a night-shift nurse. From fondling, caressing, and flattery, he gradually lured her with promises of

love and tantalized her with sexual excitement. Guilt plagued her. Yet with a childish desire to please him, she responded to his advances.

Believing that her actions helped save her parents' marriage, she continued. Her own marriage at 18 proved to be a disaster. She then joined up with another woman. "I feel more comfortable in the company of women," she commented. (Katherine Brady, *Father's Days: A True Store of Incest,* Seaview Books, pp. 58-59).

It sounds like fiction from Charles Dickens' days or from a primitive society. The reality is that this sordid affair goes on in the homes of respected citizens. Behind closed doors, children face the brutal and destructive actions of adults, mostly males, who force girls into sexual activity. Medical jargon labels it pedophilia. It is commonly known as incest.

So many private homes have been turned into playgrounds of despair. The losers are children who don't know the rules or consequences. They've been seduced onto this playground where adults, in sexual arrogance and wicked self-interest, force their victims to play their game.

The incidence of incest is so abysmal that we face an epidemic. In a study of 400 American women, the Kinsey team found 25 percent to have had a sexual experience with an adult male by 12 years of age. David Finkelhor of the University of New Hampshire, in his study of 530 female college students, reported that 19 percent had been afflicted with incest as children. If those studies reflect some sort of national average, it tells us that in the U.S., 28 million and in Canada, 2.5 million children will be so scarred ("An Epidemic of Incest," *Newsweek,* November 3, 1981).

Advocates of Incest

Not everyone laments this trend. Some people advocate incest as helpful. Organizations have been formed to encourage incest as a means of enhancing the sexual development of the child. The Rene Guyon Society recommends incestuous activity, advocating that it will help reduce divorce, drug abuse, crime, and suicide. Others suggest that intercourse between adults and children transmits affection and tenderness.

Incest occurs 95 percent of the time between an adult male and a young girl. Thus my concern in this chapter is with this group. A little girl depends on her father for life. How can she say no? He is bigger. He sustains life. Sexologists who theorize about sexual freedom need to be taken to the real world where abused girls are forced to live forever with the oppressive images of perverted men.

An adult's responsibility is to nurture children into health, not retardation; into fullness, not distortion; into integration, not perversion. Sex with a child is not only sick; it is evil.

Incest is a crime for which men try to blame their victims. Many children will not scream, protest, or be left with visible scars. Instead, they suffer endless years of self-directed anger, phobias about men and sex, and blocked channels of love and intimacy. Home, which should be a place of shared love, becomes a place of torture and hell. To an increasing proportion of the population, Daddy is a terrifying word. And the bedroom is the most dangerous place such a child can be.

Our failure to recognize incest is due to the social taboo which has acted as a barrier preventing families from talking about it. The taboo only allows it to spread. Closed doors of "good" homes retain a protective secrecy, since incest is revolting to hear about and embarrassing for those linked to it. While incestuous families may be chaotic at home, they often represent a public image of stability. If the father is known and respected, the need for secrecy is intensified.

The voice of the church is noticeably missing in condemnation of incest. Considering that up to 95 percent of incest is perpetrated by heterosexual males, why isn't a protest raised on behalf of our children? Churches are concerned with a wide variety of issues. The worldiness of amusements and lifestyles concerns some. For others, the gains of the gay movements, left-wing socialism, and Soviet aggression are of prime interest. Some focus their attention on nuclear build-up, right-wing governments, and social issues. And still others are obsessed with religious experience, wealth, and happiness.

Why do we not hear a prophetic Christian voice speaking against this gross indulgence of modern man?

Sexual Liberation

It's difficult for many of us to grasp the nature or motivation of incest. My daughter's round face peers out from under the covers, looking so lovely and at peace with the world. The possibility of her being abused fills me with revulsion. Yet for many girls, sexual abuse will be their inheritance—75 percent of reported cases are inflicted by adults the children know and trust. The closer the molester is to the family, the less likely that the incident will be reported.

Why does incest occur with such frequency today so that no family group is immune? Incest rises out of our human condition. It flows from our culture and its preoccupations. To better understand public toleration of incest, it is essential to examine the sexual dimensions of human behavior.

Sexual liberation was one of the first waves of the new morality. Many people believed that their pleasure was being restricted by the social mores of previous generations and sought for ways to reduce the hold of former thought patterns on their personal pursuits. *Playboy* publisher Hugh Heffner advocated that freedom of religion meant freedom from religion. He expressed man's freedom in terms of sexual fantasy and experience. The women's movement quickly translated this as meaning sexual freedom for themselves, as well as freedom from sexual exploitation.

Advertisers, finding that "sex sells," experimented with ads showing lusty males and seductive women. Flirtation opened the door to solicitation and finally to brazen eroticism in mass media. Society was gradually softened to permissiveness. Long-haired, noisy youth, having bought into their parents' material-ism, lost their rebellious style and became more acceptable and appealing to adults. The adult world fantasized youthfulness in its desire to stay young. Sexual appetites gone wild needed a more varied menu, and young girls added a titillating appetizer. Advertisers caught on to this delectable source of gourmet delight. Filmmakers found that seduction of childish nympho-maniacs attracted an audience. Media experts discovered that pouring youthful shapes into designer jeans sold those jeans beyond their wildest marketing projections.

The modern woman's sexual revolution has created stress among males. Men have so stereotyped women that slight departures from traditional patterns generate confusion and ambivolence. As women assert their concerns and demands, they upset the male's perception of his role.

The move by women toward equality and recognition has tremendous sexual implications. The average male has had little or no experience in dealing with the liberated woman, let alone living with one, and tends to withdraw from an ambitious and aggressive woman. However, this does not eliminate his sex drive. And so with inner anxiety and need to conquer, some men have turned on to the stimuli of young girls in films and advertising.

This perverted pursuit of sexual pleasure ignores the reality of childhood. As sexual needs are hyped and society becomes more permissive, individual and group barriers of self-control have been pushed aside. The used child has been rationalized to be a nonperson. In the crosscurrents of incestuous sexual arousal and demand, both the rights and personhood of the helpless child are forgotten. One child who suffered molestation expressed these feelings:

> I am filthy. I am sick. People get nauseated when they see me. I belong in a hole where no one can see me. I destory everything I care for. I deserve to be beaten. I was bad. I am responsible for the unhappiness of all. I am the scum of the earth. I hate every thought of me.

Incest cripples the victim with low self-esteem, depression, guilt, and sexual ambivalence. Guilt is the dominant lasting effect. She feels that somehow she is responsible or that she really did seduce the adult. The weight of anger and guilt overloads the fragile self-image.

When the child grows toward adulthood, anger builds as she recognizes that the incest happened at a time when she didn't know any better or was too vulnerable to protect herself. Fear or threats prevented her from telling anyone. Living alone for years, inside a web of feeling, she has worked her way into a stricture of loneliness.

Low self-esteem leads some girls to self-destruction. Blocking out the pain and loneliness may lead them to prostitution, drug abuse, or suicide. A study of 200 Seattle prostitutes showed that 22 percent had been sexually abused as children. Their low self-esteem led them to conclude that they were good only for delivering sexual favors.

> Each increase in my guilt, shame, and disgust caused an equal increase in my need to create a glossy pleasing surface. The darker the inside the brighter the outside must be to hide it. . . . By the time I reached high school, I had two absolutely separate personalities. The public one exhibited to family and friends alike was friendly, stable, honest, thoughtful, courteous, trust-worthy, reliable and cooperative. The private one was fearful, anxious, and depressed (Katherine Brady, *Father's Days,* pp. 58-59).

Katherine Brady describes the effect as her tender branches were damaged and broken. Love, so essential for nurture and growth, was missing. Abandoned as a child, she was forced to live outside the security and affection of parents, forever searching for faithful love and affection.

Dealing With Incest

What can an incest victim do? Who will believe her? Will she be accused of attempting to destroy her own family, especially if the home is tightly knit and the father is regarded as a faithful provider? What should the mother do? For her to admit that her husband is violating her daughter could break up the family, lose the provider, and cause untold embarrassment.

Because a girl's choice of virginity has been snatched from her, she feels set apart. She believes she is unique and can talk to no one. And if there is no one who will listen, there are no answers.

My father suffered so much from guilt after what he did to me. . . . He tried to commit suicide three times and spent a summer in a psychiatric unit. Six weeks before my marriage, he shot himself on my bed. I feel like I could have saved him a lot of suffering if I could have just told someone. But there was no way I could say the word (B. Justin and R. Justin, *The Broken Taboo (Sex in the Family)*, Human Sciences Press, p. 183).

The long-term result is that the victim feels sexually exploited by men. She sees no distinction between love and degraded sex. This can leave ugly psychological scars. She has learned from her dad to mistrust men—from the very person a little girl should be able to believe in. When she marries and then becomes a mother, her feelings continue to rush in cross-currents.

The incalculable damage of inner confusion doesn't even take into account the physical horrors.

Adult sex with children presents an increasingly serious health problem. Studies on rape have attested to the fact that infants less than a year old have been [molested]. Cases of rectal fissures, lesions, poor sphincter control, lacerated vaginas, death by asphyxiation, chronic choking from gonorrheal tonsillitis, are almost always related to adult sexual contact with children (Florence Rush, *The Best Kept Secret,* p. 6).

The adult is always at fault. He has turned to the child for selfish reasons. Regardless of any attempt to justify his behavior, he is inevitably liable. He may attempt to divest himself of responsibility. The wife may implicate the daughter by suggesting she has unwittingly seduced the male. Yet never is there justification for his actions. The child is always the victim.

Few fathers intend for incest to happen. It may start innocently enough with casual physical contact that becomes sexualized when the touch accidentally is erotic. As the touch continues, arousal takes over. For some males the motivation for incest is to experience closeness; to others it expresses hostility. A mother may unconsciously sanction the affair by silence, either believing it doesn't exist or ignoring it. Although in some cases the daughter plays to the father, this in no way legitimizes the father's actions.

In stepparent/stepchild situations, the risk factor is higher. Because there is no blood relationship, the normal taboos are weakened. If the father is under heavy stress or if intimacy with his wife is low, his need for comfort and care is not being met. In some homes incest occurs if the mother starts working at night, gets sick, or leaves a daughter and father alone too often. Violence is present about 10 percent of the time.

The mother is caught between a rock and a hard place. Even if she recognizes the problem, she may feel intimidated by the consequences in a marraige breakup, financial insecurity, and embarrassment. Also, members of the immediate or extended family may back away from dealing with the problem, fearful of upsetting the family order or of making a possible error of judgment. Even so, there is no excuse strong enough to eliminate an adult's duty to initiate action. The child needs someone to defend her. But where do you begin?

What Do You Look For?

Look for signs of abuse. With little children, a mother will notice. For older children and teenagers, look for the following indicators, remembering that taken by themselves, they are not conclusive.

- Is there a sudden and radical change in behavior?
- Are her clothes frequently torn or disturbed?
- Is there undue sexual curiosity?
- Does the child sexually playact?
- Is there refusal to do physical activity?
- Is there unexplained running away?
- Is there venereal disease?

Take the girl's confession seriously. Fear may distort the real facts, but underlying the story is something which tells you of trouble. Don't add guilt by suggesting she is imagining the situation. She may be confused as to her complicity and may even have concluded she is at fault.

Don't believe in the double standard that "Boys will be boys." Men have no more excuse for wrong sexual behavior than do women.

Remember that children are immature. Sometimes their profound insights and candor may lead you to think of them as being older. They could mislead you into assuming that children have the emotional equipment to handle the problem. The plant is still fragile.

Don't assume that the child will get over it. Ignoring it, hoping the memories and circumstances will go away, simply adds to her sense of isolation.

Resolution is required. Healing is needed. As an adult, face the fact that the process must begin and that professional help is needed.

What Does the Child Need?
The child needs to understand that she is the victim. She is not guilty. The adult is responsible and therefore guilty. This may generate anger toward the offending parent, but better that than a feeling of guilt.

She needs to hear her mother say she is not guilty. This formal declaration may be essential to future survival.

She needs to understand that incest is part of a larger problem. If she is old enough, it may help her to be told what has contributed to this breakdown.

As she relinquishes personal guilt, she needs to recognize her accountability for her actions in the future. Her acceptance that the adult was wrong could lead her to conclude that other people are always the reason for her problems. Her innocence is affirmed only in this situation.

What Should You Do?
Talk out your suspicions with a respected outsider—a doctor, minister, counselor, or phychologist. Incest is simply too explosive to deal with alone, without a third party to help you think it through objectively.

Decide who will approach the offending adult, when it will happen, and in what setting. Recognize the possible reactions, but don't be frightened off by them.

Ideally, the offender should eventually verbalize his guilt to the child and accept full responsibility.

Group therapy seems to be generally preferred for the child, rather than working it through with the child and the guilty adult. A larger group of victims, along with their supporting parents, is helpful in personal resolution.

Above all, believe that resolution and healing can come to both the child and adult. The disabling and healing of both parties can become building blocks of health and life. The past need not forever bind. The present will be changed by the hope of the future. Victims can eventually live contented married lives, experiencing sexual fulfillment.

Physical Abuse

It is tragic but true that there is a greater likelihood a woman or child will be kicked, punched, or even killed in their own homes than on the streets. Seventy percent of murders are committed by the victims' relatives or close associates. One in ten women are battered. Of every 1,000 children, one is threatened with a gun or knife by an adult, and three percent of children face serious injury by being kicked, beaten, or punched by their parents.

Family fights tend to occur on weekends, and alcohol is involved in half of these cases. Many battered wives were beaten as children and grew up associating love with physical abuse. Unemployment exacerbates the problem since stress often triggers abusive behavior. When you mix a low self-image and money problems with drugs or alcohol, the potential for violence jumps. It doesn't increase with family size, nor is it more common in any particular age or social group.

Child abuse is the most dreadful. A 34-year-old mother was convicted of manslaughter after her 14-month-old son died of a skull fracture. The ambulance drivers testified that she showed more concern for her two dogs than for the child.

A Toronto man and wife were given 15-month suspended sentences because they whipped their 15-year-old daughter with an extension cord. A three-year-old boy, weighing 13 pounds, was brought to a hospital. He should have weighed 32 pounds.

A man was sentenced to nine months for pouring alcohol

down the throat of his nine-month-old son.

Another was sentenced to two years for burning the sexual organs of his three-year-old son with a cigarette.

An adult who was abused as a child is likely to become a child abuser. The pattern of dealing with stress in violent ways is deeply ingrained. The child carries memories of being victimized over into adulthood and this establishes a pattern.

Some complexities which generate child abuse can be detected, although any one indication alone does not mean that it actually exists. These only act as indicators. Professor Greenland of McMaster University suggests that if half of the following conditions exist, action may need to be taken.

High Risk Rating List

PARENT
1. Previously abused/ neglected as a child.
2. Less than 24 at birth of first child.
3. Single parent/separated. Partner not biological parent.
4. History of abuse, neglect or deprivation.
5. Socially isolated—frequent moves—poor housing.
6. Unemployed/unskilled worker. Inadequate education.
7. Uses alcohol and/or drugs.
8. History of criminally

CHILD
1. Was previously abused or neglected.
2. Under 5 years at time of abuse.
3. Premature—or low birth weight.
4. Now underweight.
5. Birth defects—chronic illness—development lag.
6. Prolonged separation from mother.
7. Cries frequently— difficult to comfort.
8. Has difficulties in feeding

assaultive behavior
and/or suicide attempts.

9. Pregnant—just gave
birth—or chronic illness.

and elimination.

9. Adopted, foster or
stepchild.

10
Left
in Babylon

Most cults begin with a leader. Many of these have come from an evangelical heritage. Jim Jones came out of the Nazarene Church and the Disciples of Christ. Sun Myung Moon, founder of the Unification Church (Moonies), was raised in a Presbyterian missionary home in South Korea. Moses David, founder of the Children of God, came from a Christian and Missionary Alliance background. Paul Wierwille, leader of The Way International, was a Reformed Church pastor. John Robert Stevens left Pentecostalism and formed the Church of the Living Word.

We all tend to look for an apostle type leader—someone to guide us through the maze of life. It is during a time of social strife that we most readily buy into easy answers. Ron Enroth (*Lure of the Cults,* Christian Herald Books) suggests that cult leaders have three motivations:

• To exercise power so they can manipulate others in the fulfilling of their ego needs.

• To make money. This, of course, is descriptive of many religious entrepreneurs.

• To spread what they believe to be truth. Brilliance com-

122

bined with uncontrolled ego, personal charm, and charisma corners them into believing that they really do have the answers for our age.

The Call

"Come with us." Fragmented family relationships leave many young people wandering alone in large cities, not just bored but lonely. Cult recruiters can see them coming—college students in need of counseling or encouragement and someone to care.

Craig was such a student. He left his home town and moved to a West Coast city. The first two months seemed very long. Everything was different and he just couldn't strike up a friendship. One afternoon after class, he sat drinking a Coke in the college common. When two students sat down next to him, they seemed so friendly and interested. After some conversation, they invited him to a meeting that night.

He ended up going to their meeting, to hear discussion of the topic: "How to Change Violence in Our Society." Strangely, they never seemed to get around to the subject, but it didn't matter since he had a great time. Soon Craig could hardly go anywhere without one of the members coming with him. When he asked them what group they were, they didn't really say, but they sure smiled a lot. He was really hooked when he finally agreed to attend one of their weekend retreats.

For Craig, the net was carefully drawn. Emotionally he depended on their friendship, patterns of living, and their help in solving problems. For months he seemed happy but he was plagued with inner doubts. With the help of his father he finally broke away, but it took over two years for Craig to get his head together. He had to learn all over again to make decisions, to plan his day, to think about the future, and to trust his feelings.

"Desert your family." At 17, Jane was in conflict with her mom and new stepfather. The tension of living at home and being forced to attend school was more than she could stand. The Children of God suited her needs, especially when they preached that only those who "hated their fathers and mothers" could be followers of Christ.

Thousands of parents have been through the fright of teenagers being pulled away, surrounded by new "friends," subjected to brainwashing techniques, and cut off from their family and friends.

"Park your mind." The Moonies are particularly effective at answering your intellectual objections with a smile, warm enthusiasm, and affectionate acceptance. In other cults, group pressure inhibits legitimate questions. Some leaders intimidate by saying that to question them is to oppose God. Cult leader John Robert Stevens handled it this way: "You'll be taught by the Spirit what is involved in ... apostleship or you'll be left in Babylon. There is no halfway point. The only alternative you have to spiritual submission and to divine order is Babylon" (Quoted in *Eternity,* October 1979).

In his analysis of chanting in meditation, David Hadden claims that the mantra (chanting) used in Hindu, Buddhist, Islamic, and Christian mystical groups actually alters the state of the meditator. It separates words from meaning. It eliminates the thought from the mind, displaces reasoning as the means of knowing truth, and replaces the mind as the center of discovering reality. For cults, the cognitive mind becomes a barrier to further research and exploration (Spiritual Counterfeits Project Newsletter, January 1982).

"Dilute the Bible." Over the past 20 years, religions have increasingly measured faith by experience. Personal testimonies replaced discussions about truth.

Lacking an apologetic base, gospel verification soon became a matter of subjectivity. Often religious telecasts, magazines and biographies confuse the Gospel with a person's experience of the Gospel. As a consequence, our criteria for determining spirituality are often confused, subjected to the criteria of personal experience (Harold Bussell, "Beware of Cults with Their Evangelical Trappings," *Christianity Today,* March 5, 1982).

Lacking skills in evaluating a speaker's message, young people are easily swayed. Often a cult leader will build from the Scriptures, picking and choosing what is fitting to his design.

The Bible is used and the listener is not conscious of any deviation. Bussell suggests there is a pattern.

• The leader says he has found the real church.

• The leader is placed above criticism . . . his word is the final authority.

• Group sharing and testimonies are placed above Bible studies.

• The leader claims to have discovered some new spiritual insight, often centered around the last days, healing, community, or spirituality.

• The group places a high priority on living together in community.

• The group begins to develop its own language and symbols.

Why Has It Happened?

Young people didn't go beating the bushes looking for crazy religious ideas. Rather, the cults emerged at a time of unprecedented change. Everything was up for grabs. Seven factors relate to the quantum leap of religious movements in our lifetime.

• Rootlessness. "The unfocused majority" is the term Dr. R. Bibby, Sociologist at the University of Lethbridge, uses to describe religious adherents in Canada. He says their religion is without content or commitment.

THE CULTS BELIEVE

1. Jesus was one of God's incarnations.

2. The Bible is not the only authority for life.

3. There are human leaders other than Jesus through whom we get truth.

4. Jesus, although a good teacher, was not divine.

5. The Bible is a good ethical guide.

6. Only certain "enlightened" ones can interpret spiritual truth.

7. To be accepted by God, you must do something.

8. Humans are divine—they just don't know it yet.

9. By meditation we bypass our minds to meet God.

THE BIBLE TEACHES

1. God became man once, in the person of Jesus Christ, Philippians 2:6-9.

2. The Bible is God's revelation, Revelation 22:18-19.

3. Jesus is the only way to eternal life, John 14:6.

4. Jesus is God, John 1:1.

5. The Bible is inspired by God, 2 Timothy 3:16-17.

6. The Holy Spirit guides all believers, John 16:3.

7. Acceptance by God is a free gift, Ephesians 2:8-9.

8. Man is born a sinner, in need of a Saviour, Romans 3:23.

9. Knowing God renews our minds, Romans 12:2.

As well as being spiritually rootless, we are a community on wheels. Mobility pulls young people away from friends. When children leave home for college, they are separated from their families, often alone and without defined spiritual values or beliefs, open and vulnerable to new friends, new ideas, and new commitments. A broken love affair, a failed exam, a boring weekend—these can make a person an ideal candidate for a cult recruiter. Norman De Puy, commenting on the Jonestown affair said, they "did not abandon their self-control, their judgment, or their competitive instincts so much as they traded them off for love, peace, community and security" (Quoted by Ron Enroth, *Eternity*, October 1979).

• Pluralism. Religious life was predictable for most young people until 1960. Even if parents didn't go to church, most people knew what they were—Catholic, Protestant, Jewish, and occasionally a sideline religion. Within Protestantism, even if the liberals and fundamentalists didn't like each other, at least they claimed affiliation with the same God. However, immigrants brought with them their religions, gods, and ceremonies. Young people by the thousands stopped turning up at institutional churches. At the same time a growing quest for personal experience intensified interest in the mystical. As old structures tumbled, it became acceptable, even vogue, to find a religious mode, language, or experience which did something for you. Varying options filled the drab religious landscape.

• Fear of the future. The really big sellers in religious books are those describing future events—biblical prophecy or money predictions. They serve an insatiable need for a confused people who desperately hope to find out what will happen. Dr. Bibby in his study on Canadians shows that over 75 percent carefully follow their astrological predictions and over 50 percent believe their lives are influenced by their signs. Complexities of international warfare, interpersonal crises, both personal and corporate financial collapse frighten many into believing this is the end. Christian fundamentalism with its varying theories of the "end times" serves to heighten interest in this. Religious groups providing a fixed interpretation of events and a formula for predicting future events use this to sell people on membership.

• Intellectual weakness. I have seen university students, who faithfully adhere to the scientific method, leave their laboratories of research and cross the street to engage in the swooning incantations of pseudomonks who promise nonpropositional religious experience. This jump from the rational to the irrational seems to be modern man's violent rejection of science and technology.

Shaeffer saw this coming back in 1968 when he wrote, "People in our culture ... are already in process of being accustomed to accept nondefined contentless religious words and symbols without any rational or historical control. Such words and symbols are ready to be filled with the content of the moment. The words 'Jesus' or 'Christ' are the most ready for the manipulator. The phrase 'Jesus Christ' has become a content-less banner which can be carried in any direction for sociological purposes. In other words, because the phrase 'Jesus Christ' has been separated from Scripture, it can be used to trigger religiously motivated sociological actions, directly contrary to the teaching of Christ" (*The God Who Is There,* InterVarsity Press, p. 84).

In his study of cults, Ron Enroth observes that evangelical youth tend not to be well-grounded in biblical truth and thus are easily swayed by these groups. Also, new Christian converts often come from homes without religious heritage. Thus the converts have no tools to distinguish between truth and error.

• Need for heroes. For a young person it isn't just a question of who you can trust, but of who has figured out the issues and has plain and simple answers. The frightening complexities demand simplicity. Mix this need for answers with a volatile emotional quest and the results can be explosive. A charismatic leader with simple ideas, who is able to affirm who you are and tell you what to do, becomes very attractive to those starving for a religious hero. Following the leader is intuitive to man. But in a cultic context, following becomes highly exploitive.

> The religious impulse calls people from the distractions of a random world and helps them make sense of things. Religion could be called "Meaning and Belonging, Incorporated." When those who find meaning around the same vision or the same master link up, they can become dangerously intolerant (Martin E. Marty, "Religious Cause, Religious Cure," *Christian Century*, February 28, 1979).

• Authoritarianism. In 1982, hundreds of brides and grooms lined up in Madison Square Gardens to be married by Rev. Moon. Many had never before met their newly acquired spouses. Some didn't even have a common language. The matches had been neatly arranged. The confusing world with its multiplicity of choices is simplified by a father figure, often a messiah type who untangles life's knots.

Living is mapped out. Communes eliminate the need for worry over housing, food or money. But while they eliminate this stress they increasingly expand their authority in other areas. Cult members become dependent emotionally as others affirm, help them make decisions, and provide moral guidelines. The legalism and rigid moral codes of some religious groups support those who opt for the group mind. "We want heroes," comments David Gill. "We want reassurance that someone knows what is going on in this mad world. We want revolutionary folk heroes who will tell us what to do until the rapture. We massage the egos of these demagogues and canonize their every opinion. We accept without a whimper their rationalization of their errors and deviations' (Quoted by Ron

Enroth, "The Power Abusers," *Eternity,* October 1979).

● Impotence of the church. Real Christianity combines conviction, idealism, piety, self-sacrifice, discipline, obedience, and commitment. Young people influenced by the heady experiences of social activism simply aren't attracted to dead orthodoxy, insipid liberalism, or narrow fundamentalism. They look for opportunity, idealism, and challenge. Many churches caught in their own agendas have failed to recognize this pent-up need for an alive, emotionally charged, demanding faith.

Some young people turned from materialism to monasticism, since to them, comfortable Christianity offered nothing more than the old life under new titles. Theirs was "a change from affluence to poverty, from casual social relationships to strictly limited relationships, from self-direction to obedience" (J. Pankratz, "The New Monasticism," *Mennonite Brethren Herald,* January 30, 1981).

Other youth with a church heritage were challenged by the tough demands of the new groups. This offers a sad commentary on a church that fails to inspire devotion and obedience to Christ. His call is, "If anyone wishes to come after Me, let him deny himself, and take up his cross and follow Me" (Matthew 16:24).

● Search for spiritual power. Common to both Eastern and Western cults is a desire to be like God and to know the deep secrets of the universe. As Eve was lured by the serpent to seek to become as wise as God, so religions today offer seekers various means of becoming one with God and knowing the secrets of spiritual power. Frances Adeney of the Spiritual Counterfeits Project suggests that this "new age movement" has three basic tenets of belief: Because everything is one, all distinctions are an illusion. Because all is one, God is therefore one in me. Truth is perceived through a higher or altered consciousness (*His,* March 1981). She points out that EST pushes you into believing that you are God. THE WAY promises abundant living. Moses, founder of THE WAY, proclaims salvation by belonging to the perfect family. Krishna claims bad karma is dispersed by chanting. John Robert Stevens preaches that by words, reality is activated and things are spoken into existence.

None of this is really surprising. When science cannot satisfy the longing for attachment to the universe, when traditional religion fails to provide integration of truth and personal experience, young people become likely targets for religions which promise personal meaning and unity with the cosmos.

What Can Be Done?

People need answers to three primary questions:

- Who am I? Where do I fit in the cosmic order?
- What am I worth? What is my value to other people?
- Where am I going? Does today's pursuit have value for the future?

Young people have needs which deserve to be met. By understanding these needs and then creatively meeting them, in both home and church, we can strengthen our children in their faith can prevent further exodus to cults.

- Need for spiritual roots. Our spiritual roots must go down deep in the soil of biblical literature and historical Christianity. Singing current songs and having a wonderful experience may be meaningful, but faith will wither if that is all it gets.

　　—Teach the overall purposes of God by showing how His plan threads its way through the Scriptures.

　　—Show the condition of man in his desire to be like God.

　　—Stress the need for humility when it comes to discerning truth.

　　—Learn Bible verses, in context.

　　—Frequently use the inductive method of studying. Ask, What's the setting. Who wrote it? To whom? For what reason?

What does the text mean in your own words? What does it say to you in your world today?

● Need to belong. We all need to belong. The fragmenting of our society has left many young people disengaged, believing they are attached to no one. The church should provide belonging, love, accountability, and reinforcement. An unattached youth group can be dangerous. If young people only know others of their own age with similar points of view, they can easily fall into a one-track group mind. They need the full body of Christ in their area.

● Need for security. The uncertainties of vocation, marriage, global concerns, and personal success leave many searching for simple solutions. One such trap in the church is a simplistic eschatology. Overpreoccupation with end times, at the expense of daily nurture and obedience to Christ, can misrepresent the real nature of Christ's plan for the future. Because of the inordinate interest our culture has in defining future events, we must be careful not to grasp at popular theories which offer easy answers. Christ's call is to faithfulness.

Christ's coming is imminent (at any time) but not necessarily immediate (now). The future is held by Christ, not by any national or religious leader.

● Need to think. I have heard Christian youth leaders putting down education. This is sad, because God wishes to use thoughtful minds. We need to cultivate a careful balance in our youth of trained minds and believing hearts. Granted, it is easier for kids to listen to someone with all the answers. But leaders are responsible for building into young minds the ability to sort through various ideas and experiences, to set them against Scripture, to screen out what is error. Remember Paul's timeless affirmation? "And do not be conformed to this world but be transformed by the renewing of your mind, that you may prove what the will of God is, that which is good and acceptable and perfect" (Romans 12:2).

• Need for ideals. Young people seem to have a built-in predisposition to idealism. As they see greed, nationalism, broken families, and a cluttered society, they want to do something about them. The tough demands cults make are attractive to many. Cults follow leaders, believing that through their group they will change the world.

Responsible obedience to the claims of Christ demands full commitment. We must carefully teach, challenge, and lead our youth into a lifestyle which is in line with the will of Christ.

For More Information About Cults

BOOKS

Cults, World Religions and You, Kenneth Boa, Victor Books
Escape from Darkness, Compiled by James R. Adair and Ted Miller, Victor Books
The Kingdom of the Cults, Bethany Fellowship Press
The Lure of the Cults, Ronald Enroth, Christian Herald Books
The New Cults, Walter Martin, Vision House
Prison or Paradise—The New Religious Cults, James and Marcia Rudin, Fortress Press
Scripture Twisting—20 Ways the Cults Misread the Bible, James Sire
Youth, Brainwashing, and the Cults, Zondervan

ORGANIZATIONS

Acts 17
Box 2183
La Mesa, CA 92041

American Family Foundation, Inc.
P.O. Box 343
Lexington, MA 02173

Campus Ministry Communications
Lutheran Council in the USA
35 East Wacker Dr., 1847
Chicago, IL 60601

Institute of Contemporary Christianity
Box A
Oakland, NJ 07436

Spiritual Counterfeits Project
P.O. Box 2418
Berkeley, CA 94702
415 548-7949—hotline for immediate information
Write for the Newsletter and SCP Journal.

EDUCATION RESOURCES

Cults, World Religions and You, Leader's Guide, Victor Books
Distinctions: Christian Replies to World Philosophies, David
Sheffel and Mike Roeder, David C. Cook, Lifestyle Series
Traps: A Probe of Those Strange New Cults, Harris Langford,
The Presbyterian Church in America

Specific Steps You Can Take to Lift the Siege

Understand the Issues

1. Note statistics, trends, and ideas coming from your reading and from local and national news sources.
2. Meet with parents of your children's friends. Take an evening to discuss what each is observing and learning. Don't confine yourself to those who believe just as you do. Get a wide range of ideas.
3. Ask the Christian Education department of your church to set up study sessions on contemporary youth issues. Invite those who work with youth, in church and the community.
4. Learn to interpret the trends of youth within your own setting. National trends may not exactly fit your area, but don't conclude your area is free of them just because you haven't encountered them.
5. Learn from professionals engaged in youth work, but don't be intimidated by them. After all, you raise your children. You are the one who has to make it all work at home.

Move into Action

1 Get to know the ministry groups in your schools and the agencies, both Christian and secular, who work with young people. Find ways to help them. Get involved. Become a volunteer. Help them raise their budgets. By caring, you will help them and charge your life for service.
2. Meet the leaders in the political and educational structures of your community. Find out what they stand for and cordially remind them you hold them accountable for their leadership.
3. Watch for some of the signs I've suggested in this book. Your neighbors may be experiencing stress and need someone to care. Don't pretend you have all the answers. The very act of

showing they matter will ease the gripping fear that they are all alone.

4. Start something. For example if you find there are many battered wives or children who have no place to go, open a shelter. In researching, you may find a national or regional group who can help you with your plans.

5. Remember that this is God's world. We can't sweep away the tough issues with a neat religious phrase. Life isn't that way. But life does have purpose. Even if you don't recognize God's care for you, He's still there. Open your life to His wisdom and guidance. Building your life on His truth will give you a reliable foundation. And you then can give your children the spiritual ingredients necessary for healthy bodies, minds, and spirits.

OTHER VICTOR BOOKS YOU WILL WANT TO READ

A Mother's Touch
   Elise Arndt

How to Really Love Your Child
   Ross Campbell, M.D.

How to Really Love Your Teenager
   Ross Campbell, M.D.

How to Disciple Your Children
   Walter A. Henrichsen

A Man's Touch
   Charles F. Stanley

How Does Your Marriage Grow?
   Bartlett and Margaret Hess

The Power Delusion
   Anthony Campolo, Jr.

The Power of a Positive Self-Image
   Clifford G. Baird